THE ABSURDITY OF ATHEISM

How Science, History and Reason Show That Atheism is Absurd

Second Edition Expanded

Gerald Charles Tilley, PHD

California Biblical University Press

P.O. Box 1520

Tustin, CA 92781

Published in the USA

Copyright 2014 by Gerald Charles Tilley

Second Edition Expanded 2018

All Rights Reserved

Cover: Hubble Telescope   April 2005 (STScl-2005-12)
Courtesy of NASA, ESA, S. Beckwith (STScl), and the Hubble Heritage Team (STScl)

TABLE OF CONTENTS

Explanatory Note to the Second Edition .... Page 4

Part I

Introduction .... Page 5
What is Atheism? .... Page 10
Atheism and the Reformation .... Page 13
How Common Is Atheism? .... Page 16
False Explanations .... Page 17
Goals and Methods of Atheism .... Page 19
The Evolution-Creation Debate .... Page 20
Atheism Becomes Anti-Human .... Page 24
Censorship by Atheists .... Page 28
Claims Atheism Elevates Humanity .... Page 30
The New Atheism? .... Page 32
Atheist's Strategies .... Page 34
More Atheistic Faith Assumptions .... Page 38
Christian Theism and Muslim Violence .... Page 42
Additional Atheistic Strategies .... Page 45
Why Atheism Is More Dangerous Now .... Page 47
Why Bother to Refute Atheism? .... Page 50
Refuting the Methods of Atheism .... Page 52
Arguments from Silence .... Page 56
Self-Refuting Statements .... Page 60
The Reality of Pain and Evil .... Page 62
Scientific Arguments for Atheism .... Page 65
The Argument of Vestigial Organs .... Page 69
Microevolution is Not Macroevolution .... Page 71
Atheism is Held By Faith .... Page 75
Evaluating Arguments .... Page 75
Intolerance of Atheists .... Page 79
The Origin of Intelligent Design .... Page 84

Part II
Refuting Atheism & Evolution With Science

- Cosmology .... Page 87
- Geology: Pleochroic Halos .... Page 90
- The Anthropic Principle .... Page 91
- No Science in a Random Universe .... Page 93
- Entropy Contradicts Evolution .... Page 94
- Spontaneous Generation Disproved .... Page 95
- Design and Irreducible Complexity .... Page 98
- Lack of Fossil Evidence .... Page 102
- Evidence From Health Sciences .... Page 107
- Refuting Atheistic Propaganda .... Page 111
- Atheists Switching Definitions .... Page 112
- Responding to Atheists .... Page 114
- Summary of the Evidence .... Page 117

Some Former Atheists .... Page 119
Concluding Statements .... Page 122

Resource Endnotes .... Page 124
Recommended Bibliography: Books .... Page 149
Articles, Pamphlets, Internet .... Page 150
Name/Author Index .... Page 151

Explanatory Note to the Second Edition Expanded

This new edition corrects a few inadvertent misspellings of names and a few other typos in the first edition. It also includes extensive rewriting, and extensive additional content. Some endnotes have been expanded and others added. The endnote numbers have been bolded and enlarged to make them easier to distinguish. An author/name index is added. Margins have been diminished to include the extra information without excessively adding to the total pages. The original bibliography has been cut down to only recommended items since all referenced material is in the endnotes.

Part I

Introduction

In his introduction to a symposium in 1995 examining the atheist and Christian worldviews, Georges Carillet stated, *"All knowing begins in believing, in trusting someone and something to be true. Even the lauded 'empirical method' of the hard sciences begins in this way!"*

[1]It is well known that one's presuppositions that is, what one assumes to be foundational truth, often determines the results of one's research or analysis even when contradicted by the evidence itself. Such assumptions greatly affect what we believe to be true and can determine our conclusion before any evaluation occurs. One's presuppositions are often unexamined and even largely unrecognized.

Those presuppositions may also be misleading and thereby prevent the individual from recognizing truth or reality despite research and investigation of truth claims. The ability to separate truth from falsehood may also be lacking due to one's erroneous presuppositions.

In his book, <u>Attacking Faulty Reasoning</u> T. Edward Damer states, *"But as critical thinkers, we must be honest about this information and thus not discount it simply because it comes into conflict with our own opinions ... "*[2]

Following up on that insight, Roger Baker wrote *"... one does not avoid bias by denying its existence but rather by recognizing openly and honestly what that bias is ...* Clearly laying out assumptions as differentiated from facts all serve to help overcome bias ... "*[3] **These observations are essential to recognize, especially when we are involved in investigating truth claims.**

Major assumptions Theists make that atheists deny are: That God exists and is just and good; that God acts in history and always has good or just (moral) reasons for His actions; that He can raise people from the dead. This book has the further assumptions that atheism is unbelievable and absurd because it proves to be without either genuine scientific or other rational basis. The author further believes the Christian Faith to be authentic, true and intellectually defensible.

My friend Georges Carillet expressed my thinking and the purpose of this book well when he wrote, *"For some of us, Christianity has been chosen not because it is 'useful' or 'successful'- but because it is true. Darwin, Freud and Marx have misled us for so long that this very statement seems so archaic, so 'unscientific,' even arrogant. But it is a statement that deserves honest examination using the best tools of modern scientific and historical research,"*[4]

In order to give a fair hearing to the evidence presented in this book, you are being asked to become aware of your presuppositions and bias's in regard to both atheism and the Christian Faith. You are asked to temporarily set them aside to objectively evaluate the presentation. At the end then compare your prior assumptions with the evidence that has been presented to determine which seems more valid.

In <u>A Thirst For Meaning</u> Calvin Miller mentions that a some skeptics complain that they sought the truth and examined the evidence but were unconvinced. Though the skeptic may have been sincere, *"it is usually obvious that he has not abandoned his presuppositions before he began his search."*[5]

To repeat the significance of this; the person's prior assumptions (presuppositions) determine the results in advance of checking the evidence, unless he or she identifies those presuppositions and put them on hold. Without questioning his prior assumptions, the skeptic's investigation will most likely be a waste of time.

Some might question the appropriateness of the title, <u>The Absurdity of Atheism</u>. After all, some brilliant men and women have been atheists. However, mere intelligence proves nothing. People of great intelligence have also been Bahia's, Buddhists, Confucianists, Christians, Deists, Hindus, Jews, Muslims, Parsees and about everything else imaginable.

These beliefs greatly contradict each other and cannot all be true. So intelligence alone is no proof one is on the correct path, nor that one is in the pursuit of truth. Motives and desires are certainly as important as intelligence. There must be the will to examine and follow the evidence as well as to embrace the truth to which the evidence leads. Many people, if not most seem content to remain in the beliefs in which they were raised rather than attempting to verify the truth or falseness of their views.

Relevant to the title of this publication is the statement of former atheist Paudge Mulinhill of Ireland, *"I was to discover that there are a number of serious problems with atheism, a number of significant facts that leave it without a leg to stand on … both science and the laws of logic contradicted atheism."*[6]

A further issue that must be cleared up is the false claim that faith and reason are opposite foundations for belief, or that they are contrary to each other. All philosophical and religious beliefs, including atheism, are held by faith in the presuppositions or assumptions one has about reality. That set of assumptions form the foundation for one's worldview.

It has been said that the mind cannot be proven to be rational, but that this must be assumed in order to prove anything else. Reason then is not a separate mental faculty in contrast to faith. Instead it is the faculty used by those of any belief system to understand, explain, promote and defend that belief system.

John Blanchard explains, *"It is no exaggeration to say we live by faith, in that it influences every part of our lives. Whenever we make a decision about anything, even the smallest everyday thing, we believe not only that we have valid reasons for doing so, but that we are qualified to say such reasons are valid. Relying upon reason itself is an act of faith."*[7]

Faith is the foundation for one's use of reason and reason is the basis of defending one's faith. This is true regardless of what it is that one actually believes. However, all reasoning is not of equal validity or strength. Some person's reasoning skills are highly developed and others are not. Some reasoning is based upon emotional convictions and some upon evidence. Some individual's reasoning is more logical and consistent than others.

In her article "Roots of Science Denial", Katherine Hayhoe wrote, "*The only way to have a constructive dialogue with a dismissive person is on the level at which he or she really has the issue.*"[8] It therefore makes sense to attempt to find out what the actual issue is with a particular person professing atheism. For some it is a reaction due to some tragic event or horrible experience connected with religion. There are others who deny the existence of God in order to justify their lifestyle. The fallacy there is assuming one's wishes or preferences can create or alter reality. Another major cause for atheism is intellectual pride.

Cyril Joad spent his career as a philosophy professor dedicated to destroying Christianity. After his conversion to Christ he wrote, "*There is such a thing as pride of the intellect, a pride in which throughout my life I have been continuously proud.*"[9] He further stated that the pride of intellect was the major reason modern intellectuals find it difficult to believe in God.[10] This last point will come up again near the end of this presentation.

Like the origin of my first book, (The Uniqueness of the Christian Faith), this one began as a series of lectures. My travels in Western and Eastern Europe has given me opportunities to hear and read material from scientists from both parts of Europe and the former Soviet Union. Most of these scientists are former atheists. My exposure to, and referencing of these scientists adds uniqueness and value to this book.

Another motive to publish relates to an experience from years ago. I overheard two students answering objections to the Christian faith made by two others. As their objections were answered, the critics moved on to new arguments. They finally ran out of criticisms and returned to ones that they had used earlier. At this point I interrupted and said something like, "*It's obvious you are not intellectually honest since you are returning to criticisms that were answered previously.*" The critics left shortly thereafter.

This is a familiar experience of those who defend Christian Theism. Once time has elapsed, critics revive old claims and arguments that have been thoroughly refuted. But few people read older books. The critics either do not know the arguments have been refuted, or rely upon people having short memories. Critics assume old books are irrelevant even when the evidence has never been refuted and is therefore still reliable.

Former atheist, Alister McGrath who has doctorates in molecular biophysics and Theology, refers to a non-existent quote he finally got Richard Dawkins to quit using. *"Dawkins had fallen into the trap of not checking his sources and merely repeating what older atheist writers had said. It's yet another wearisome example of the endless recycling of outdated arguments that has become so characteristic of atheism in recent years."*[11]

Continued scientific discoveries are making atheism and evolution less and less tenable. Despite this, proponents of these concepts make confident assertions that mislead many. It's important to recognize that assertions are not proof and sarcasm and ridicule do not replace or refute evidence.

Sam Harris for example asked *"how is it that in this one area of our lives, we have convinced ourselves that our beliefs about the world can float entirely free of reasons and evidence?"*[12] **While true in regard to the world religions, it is certainly not true in regard to the Christian Faith, which is well supported by both and which invites the examination of its sources and evidence.**

For these reasons it is essential to publish new books that once again expose false ideas and refute new variations of invalid arguments. It is also important to present new scientific information that demolishes false assumptions.

A few of the scientists who are destroying the credibility of atheism and evolution: Australian microbiologist, Michael Denton, Evolution: A Theory in Crisis; Mathematician and philosopher, William Dembski, Intelligent Design; Molecular chemist, Michael Behe, Darwin's Black Box: The Biochemical Challenge to Evolution; German Information Scientist and Engineer, Werner Gitt, In The Beginning Was Information; Biologist, Jonathan Wells, Icons of Evolution: Science or Myth?; Physicist, Hugh Ross, Why The Universe Is the Way It Is; Chemist, Henry F. Schaefer III, Science and Christianity: Conflict or Coherence?; and biologist, Stephen C. Meyer, Signature In the Cell: DNA and the Evidence for Intelligent Design.

Intelligent Design is sometimes referred to as ID. Many other scientists and scholars who effectively expose the absurdity of atheism and macroevolution will be referred to in the content and endnotes of the following pages.

I have sought to track down every quote and apologize in advance for any oversight. I thank my wife, Nancy and my son Trent for editing and helpful ideas on the first edition. Dennis Black has been of great assistance in various ways for each of my books. Any errors are, of course my own responsibility.

What is Atheism?

There is a story of two little boys who were always getting into trouble in their small town. Whenever anything bad happened there everyone was sure these boys had caused it.

Finally, in desperation their mother asked the local minister if he would see if he could get them to change. He agreed, but said he wanted to see the younger boy alone first. The minister was behind his huge desk. The boy came in and sat down. He was very scared not knowing what was going to happen.

The minister looked at the boy and in a loud voice said 'Where is God?' The confused boy didn't know what to say. The minister leaned forward and repeated louder, 'WHERE is God?' The boy was now too terrified to speak. The minister leaned over the desk, practically touching the boy with his pointing finger and shouted, 'WHERE IS GOD?'

The boy jumped up and ran out the door to his older brother sobbing, 'We're really in trouble this time.' 'Why?' his brother asked. He replied, 'Because God is missing and they think it's our fault!'

Like the little boy, some people think God is missing from the universe, absent, or non-existent, but, they are mistaken. They have misinterpreted the phenomenon of the universe and the experiences of their own senses.

Renowned philosopher and historian Will Durant declared: "*The greatest question of our time is ... whether men can live without God.*"[13] In answer to the question we can look at previous and current examples of societies based upon atheism. These examples do not give hope for a positive outcome if atheism triumphs in the U.S. or other additional nations. If previous attempts to live and base a culture upon atheism have continued relevance, the outlook for humanity is not good.

The literal meaning of atheism today is "no God." This agrees with most modern usage of the term. An atheist believes that all of existence can be explained by natural processes. In other words, that there is no such thing as the supernatural. They assume nature is all there is.

Atheist Richard Dawkins explains that an atheist, *"believes there is nothing beyond the natural physical world, no supernatural creative intelligence lurking behind the observable universe, no soul that outlasts the body and no miracles – except in the sense of natural phenomena that we don't yet understand."*[14]

Josh McDowell writes, *"An atheist is convinced that all religious belief, evidence and faith are false."*[15] **C.S. Lewis wrote in <u>Mere Christianity:</u>** *"When I was an atheist I had to try to convince myself that most of the human race have always been wrong about the question that mattered to them most ..."*[16]

11

The term, atheism, can also refer to one who does not believe in a personal God. In this case atheistic would mean not theistic. The non-theist might, believe in some concept of a god or creative force. Deism is a more accurate term to refer to belief in a non-personal Creator. Deism is defined as "*belief in the existence of a supreme being arising from reason rather than revelation.*"[17] Deists accept that God is revealed through nature but not through scripture. Deism better describes the thinking of some often mistakenly categorized as atheists, such as Voltaire.

Deists believe that God created the universe but is not interested in humanity. They think it is impossible to have a connection or relationship with that God.[18] That would seem to possibly be a small step closer to reality. However, consider whether it is rational to believe a God would create beings who are interested in Him, if He has no interest in them. Why would He bother to do so? Deism is not a satisfactory alternative.

The premise of The Absurdity of Atheism is that the denial of the existence of God is not verifiable, not scientific, nor reasonable. This book contends that the evidence strongly supports the conclusion that God is the ultimate reality and that it makes sense to reject atheism as absurd.

Some atheists prefer the label secular humanists. Another form of atheism is Marxism also known as Communism. There are also many who live as if there is no God, though they might deny the label. Each version is the denial of God's existence.

According to Oxford professor Alister McGrath, originally, "*the Greek term atheistos meant something like 'one who denies the traditional religion of the Athenian establishment.'*"[19]

Atheism was much less common in ancient times. No government or educational system sought to brainwash the populace to believe it. No media or intellectuals sought to convince people that God did not exist. The advocacy of atheism has increased dramatically since the 18th century.

Those who claimed to be atheists in earlier times were like Socrates. Their atheism was a reaction to and rejection of the pagan gods. These gods were limited in knowledge and power, or limited as to their particular sphere of authority. They were in continual conflict with each other and their immoral behavior was as bad as or worse than most mortals.[20] The actions of these so-called gods revealed their merely human origin.

Those who rejected these man-made gods were called atheists. Atheism then was always an individual choice to reject the religion of one's own social group.[21]

During early church history, in the Roman Empire, Christians were often called atheists. They denied the existence of pagan gods and rejected the Emperor's claim to be God. The rejection of these pagan claims was sometimes misinterpreted as atheism.[22]

Atheism and the Reformation

The significance of atheism has greatly changed since ancient times. During the Middle Ages the Christian Faith and European society became contaminated with all kinds of superstition and magical thinking. The Renaissance began to challenge the validity of such things and some philosophers proposed that they could satisfactorily explain the existence of man and the universe without God. These Renaissance thinkers were the first in modern times to identify themselves as atheists.[23] Atheism did not, however, gain prominence until the eighteenth century.

The massive religious and intellectual changes that grew out of the Protestant Reformation of the sixteenth century were significant in aiding the rise of modern atheism.[24] Because of the success of the Reformation, there were now options one could consider regarding belief in God.[25]

The Reformation resulted in the reclamation of the use of one's mind in regard to matters of faith. Now superstitions accumulated over the centuries could be rejected without rejecting God or Christianity.

The appeal of atheism in Europe was primarily as a means of diminishing the excessive power and control of the Church. Opposition to the church was increasing because it had largely become a vehicle of exploitation and oppression[26]

McGrath informs us, *"Paradoxically, the historical origins of modern atheism lie primarily in an extended criticism of the power and status of the church, rather than in any asserted attractions of a godless world."*[27]

It was thought that the most effective means of reducing the Church's power was to undermine the credibility of its teachings. As this quest proceeded atheism began to develop philosophical and cultural sophistication.[28]

A huge factor in justifying and promoting atheism came from redefining reality. Unbelieving scholars declared the universe to be a vast eternal machine functioning according to natural laws. They assumed the universe to be a closed system, which would eliminate any supernatural involvement or intervention. These assumptions excluded the need for and possibility of a Creator. God's existence had not been refuted. Reality had merely been redefined in such a way as to exclude Him.[29] The assumptions of these scholars became taught as if they were facts; God had officially become a superstition.

James I. Packer considers the forms of atheism in the West as a reaction against Christianity and therefore produced by Christianity. In explanation he writes:

"Atheism is essentially anti-theism, a negation of theism, a reaction against someone else's belief in God. Therefore it is a chameleon, taking its colour from the sort of faith in God that it denies. All the atheisms that the world has ever seen have been reactions against some prior form of belief in God or gods."

"It could be shown that the other atheisms of Christian history [in addition to Marxism] have also been built out of re-angled Christian concepts and secularized Christian ideals."[30]

Atheism in practice opposes and distorts the source of its best ideals. Atheism has stolen biblical concepts such as the worth and dignity of man and claimed these values come, not from God, but from eliminating God. Atheism and the other religions of man are all distortions and departures from the original knowledge of the one true God. Various anthropologists have verified from research into tribes from all over the world that monotheism was the original belief of mankind.[31]

Former Marxist, Ignace Lepp agrees with attributing modern atheism to Christianity: *"...it is precisely the purest and most sublime religion, even by admission of its adversaries that has given rise to the most virulent and the most generalized form of atheism."*[32]

Lepp goes on to say that some modern atheists began by attempting to confront and renew the superficial pretense of Christianity in their European culture. Their efforts were strongly resisted and failed. Their lack of success at reform led them to gradually *"renounce and oppose Christianity itself and, finally, religion as such."*[33] He explains that since those would be reformers saw Christianity as the most excellent religion, once they abandoned it, there was nowhere to go but to complete unbelief.

Packer points out that the Bible presents us with two types or levels of atheism, the practical and the theoretical. Practical atheism is living as if there is no God. Practical atheism is the way of life of the majority of people in the West. Theoretical atheism is the assertion that God does not exist.

The first humans established this pattern of wanting "*to be as God knowing good and evil.*" They desired to be wise enough to not need God. According to Packer practical atheism is a universal impulse of man and the foundation of theoretical atheism[34] In other words, practical atheism is natural to everyone.

Atheism seeks to establish the idea of man being his own god. Packer quotes the Bible at Romans 1:21, "Knowing God, they *refused to honor him as God*" **and explains this attitude makes the next step into complete denial of God's existence quite easy.**[35]

In the modern West, theoretical atheism appears in the name of humanity as a reaction against theism (belief in a personal God). Theism is claimed to be a tyrannical enslavement to superstition and myth.

How Common Is Atheism?

It is difficult to determine how many atheists there are in the world. Though atheism is the designated ideology in some nations, it is uncertain how many people in those regions actually believe it. Another cause for uncertainty as to the actual number of atheists is because there are differing conceptions of just what qualifies as atheism.[36]

A poll published in 2006 shows the percentages of self-reported atheism varies greatly but is highest in Western Nations. Following are the reported percentages for several countries *"United States (4%), Italy (7%), Spain (11%) Great Britain (17%), Germany (20%) and France (32%)."* [37]

A 2007 editorial in <u>Christianity Today</u> reported that: *"Atheists may be a minority (from 8 to 27 percent of the American population depending upon the poll and the questions asked), but they tend to dominate elite institutions."*[38]

The fact that atheists tend to dominate elite institutions such as scientific organizations and science journals, Deans of University Science Departments etc., gives them prominence and influence far beyond their actual numbers.

To repeat, the situation is much different today than in ancient times. Atheism is much more common and widespread today because of deliberate promotion, especially in our Universities. Ignace Lepp the French Psychotherapist converted from Marxism states:

"*Contemporary atheism, at least in the developed countries of Christian civilization, is distinguished from the atheism of other times and other civilizations above all by its extension. It is no longer a phenomenon of a few individuals protesting against society. ..."*[39]

Whole societies have been subjected to propaganda and brainwashing to convince them of atheism. Famous authors have also popularized atheism. The intellectual elite, the mainstream media and secular Universities of the West have largely bought into the myth of atheism as well.

False Explanations

Atheism especially targets Christianity and the God of the Bible for its attacks. Ignace Lepp writes that it is *"The Christian religion which almost all atheists see as the obstacle to their idea of man and his happiness."*[40]

In an effort to explain why the vast majority of humans have some type of religious orientation, *"Atheistic philosophers, sociologists and psychologists have elaborated numerous theories and hypotheses in an effort to give a plausible scientific explanation of the universality of religious phenomena."*[41]

These explanations began in 1841 after publication of Ludwig Feuerbach's <u>The Essence of Christianity</u>. He completely discredited the Christian faith as well as all religion. Since then, most atheists have attributed religious belief to the psychological projection of one's needs as Feuerbach had declared.[42] Feuerbach greatly influenced Marx, Engles, Nietzsche, Freud, Sartre and others in their opposition to Christianity.[43]

Feuerbach's explanation suited the preferences of these thinkers. As a result they popularized the idea that Christianity (and all belief in God) was mistaken; that God only exists in the mind of those who believe.

Such explanations are frequently true. It is obvious that conflicting concepts of God cannot all be accurate. There are many ideas about God that are false, existing only in the mind of those who believe such mistaken ideas.

However, even when belief in God is a projection of one's needs, that does not disprove God's existence. The need of such persons merely explains why they embrace belief. Even if a specific concept of God is false, that does not prove there is no God. Feuerbach was wrong. These arguments are invalid, having no bearing on whether God exists or not. In fact, the arguments only exists in the mind as well so that would be sufficient reason to dismiss such argument. Also, would it not make sense that a genuine God who created humanity would meet some human psychological needs?

The arguments of Feuerbach, however were used to justify claims that belief in God was a dangerous delusion to be fought and eradicated. Religion was asserted to be the cause of all human problems by such men as Nietzsche, Marx, and Freud.[44]

Similarly, believers often assume that those who choose atheism in the West do so out of some psychological need. One such need is to justify their lifestyle.[45] In many cases this is true. These atheists are attempting to convince themselves they are not accountable to a supreme being in order to justify their choices. This is a misguided determination to be totally free; free of any absolute values or inconvenient moral restraints; the desire to be God.[46] This is the basis for the atheism of some, but such motives do not disprove atheism.

Another assumption about atheists is that they had a troubled or non-existent relationship with their father. It is also often assumed, *"that the atheist only knows a false form of religion."*[47] Both have often been true. But even when true, these causes do not prove atheism to be false, they merely show why certain individuals have embraced it.

There are those who reject the existence of God out of reaction to the suffering, pain, evil and injustice in the world. They assume God would not allow such things if He existed, or that any God who would allow such things would either be powerless to control evil or be evil himself. This ignores that most evil and suffering is clearly the result of human choices and actions. (More on this later). So both sides in the God debate tend to dismiss the serious thinking and beliefs of the other.

As frequently stated, the vast majority of mankind is incurably religious. Lepp states that this characteristic of humanity is recognized even by atheists and that many atheists accept Voltaire's opinion that, for the masses, religion is necessary.[48] It is becoming obvious that atheism and evolution are like alternative religions for some people. Those theories are often held with religious tenacity despite lack of confirming data.[49] Could it be that religion reveals that humans were created with the capacity and need to worship God?

It is noteworthy that despite extreme measures over many years, Russia and China have been unsuccessful at eradicating belief in God. In fact religion within those countries is widespread and increasing in recent decades.

Goals and Methods of Atheism

Leaders of some nations have used atheism to justify actions which could not be defended were they to acknowledge accountability to God. Dostoevsky aptly expressed this attitude in **The Brothers Karamazov**: "*If there is no God, everything is permissible.*"

An article about Dostoevsky relates that "*In and through his unforgettable characters, Dostoevsky demonstrates how one's free choice in believing or rejecting God will have profound consequences of a moral and ethical nature.*"[50]

When atheism became the ideology adopted by a nation's political leaders, the results were the atrocities of the French Revolution, Fascism, Marxism and the Nazi regime and all the consequences of those movements. The result of atheistic beliefs in each nation that has adopted atheism has been brutal regimes that murder their own people.[51] This is because once atheism is the official ideology people only exist for the purposes of the state and for reproduction. Humans cannot have inherent value nor inalienable rights in an atheistic society.

Robert Morey warned that it is important to pay attention to what happened in Russia, China, Cuba, etc. when the communists took over. Why? Because atheists in the West are removing public expression of belief as was done in Communist nations.[52] Atheists are using the same methods here to eliminate religion as were and are used in those atheistic nations.

In the U.S. atheists have largely succeeded in removing evidence of God from academia. They seek to eliminate all evidence of God from the marketplace, and media as well. Atheists use the courts and threats of lawsuits to achieve the removal of public displays and expressions of faith in God.

Some atheist authors are even rewriting past history to eliminate evidence of God and the influence of faith in Him. This is another deceptive tactic the communists used after taking over Russia. They created a predominately false picture of Russia's past. Thus we see that in the promotion of the ideology of atheism, truth, reality and integrity often become early casualties.

If Atheists are willing to distort the past to deceive us, why should we not expect them to do the same in the present? This willingness to deceive means we can expect more examples of false claims and forged evidence and other distortions of reality. Past examples of this willingness to deceive are Haeckel's faked drawings of the human embryo;[53] misleading visual portrayals in science textbooks of alleged human evolution from a missing ancestor;[54] the reconstructions of fossil finds;[55] the alleged human tooth used in the Scopes trial,[56] the disproven declaration of vestigial organs in humans[57] and the well-known 'Piltdown Man Hoax.'[58] There has been a number of other fake fossils as well.[59]

The Evolution-Creation Debate

This issue clearly shows the goal and methods of many atheists. When atheists desired to oppose the teaching of creation in our schools, they asserted that students should hear evolution taught as well as creation. They stated that teachers should have the academic freedom to present alternative views.

Once allowed to present evolution, they sought to eliminate any mention of arguments and evidence for creation. They falsely argued that creation was merely a religious perspective and therefore had no place in science classes. Thus scientific evidence for creation was removed from courses. Only one interpretation of the scientific data is now allowed; that of evolution. Most atheists completely ignore, deny and distort the scientific information that does not validate evolution or that contradicts their theories.

Creation scientists are denied the very rights atheists demanded. Clarence Darrow, arguing for the inclusion of evolution, had stated that to present only one view of origins was bigotry.[60] It still is!

Scientific Creationism and Intelligent Design are both excluded from the public schools and state universities. Science teachers and professors have been terminated for attempting to retain a true atmosphere of academic freedom in their classrooms. The claim that creationism and intelligent design are without any genuine scientific basis is dishonest.

William Dembski wrote that, *"The design theorists' critique of Darwinism begins with Darwinism's failure as an empirically adequate theory, not with its supposed incompatibility with some system of religious belief."*[61]

Robert Morey stated that if it were actually true that creation had no scientific basis, the fastest way to discredit creation and religion would be to allow scientific advocates of creation or intelligent design to present their views, but this approach is usually fought and prevented.[62]

As often stated, *"... obviously, truth can stand for itself if it is given a fair hearing."*[63] **A fair hearing is precisely what evolutionists seek to prevent because the flaws in evolution are then seen and the strength of the scientific evidence for Creation becomes apparent.**

Rarely are both sides of the evolution debate presented in the media or classroom When it does occur, there is an obvious stacking the deck against creation. The evolutionist is someone with recognized scientific credentials. The creationist is usually a minister or other person without such credentials and expertise. This promotes the false ideas that no genuine scientists reject evolution and that belief in a Creator is without any scientific or rational basis. The mainstream media presents a warped view of both creation and evolution.

There are many scientists who would gladly present evidence contrary to evolution. They are, however, regularly excluded from such opportunities. To gain a hearing for scientists who believe in Creation, some Creationist or Intelligent Design group must normally organize their own presentations. These are generally ignored or misrepresented by the media. February 7, 2014 the TV news program, "Nightline" Informed us of a debate between anti-evolutionist Ken Ham and William Nye, "The Science Guy" from TV. Ham had been a High School science teacher decades ago.

The program included a very brief excerpt of the debate. Attempting to discredit those opposing evolution, Nye made the claim that opposition or disagreement with evolution only exists in the United States. This as well as other statements Nye made are completely false, as the endnote shows.[64]

Evolutionists reject allowing scientists who are Creationists or Intelligent Design advocates from presenting their perspective in classrooms. This is because these scientists present evidence ignored by evolutionists; because they demonstrate credibility as genuine scientists and provide genuinely scientific evidence contrary to evolution.

Scientists who believe in creation or ID also expose the weakness of arguments and lack of actual evidence for evolution. It's easier to refute the truncated arguments of those who are not in the classroom, than to refute the presentation of a non-evolutionary scientist who is present.

The one present can refute 'straw man' arguments and false claims.

Milton Steinberg wrote, *"This then is the scientific reason for believing in God; that though this belief is not free from difficulties, it stands out head and shoulders, as the best answer to the riddle of the universe."*[65] **Though in agreement with Steinberg's statement, there are also other scientific reasons for believing in God. Many of those reasons will be presented and explained.**

Atheists seek to eliminate any opportunity to hear or discover evidence for creation or the existence of God. Ultimately, the true purpose of "the new atheism" is not to discover the truth but to eliminate all religion and religious beliefs from society.[66]

Aldus Huxley admitted a non-scientific reason behind his dogmatic claims for evolution and atheism. He expressed a strong desire to eliminate the moral restraints of religion.[67] **Evidently, then personal desires, and preferences often influence the beliefs of some scientists and philosophers more than actual facts.**

Anti-religion propaganda and tactics are proving effective. Profession of atheism is becoming far more common. Decades ago the popular stance was to claim belief in God or that you were searching for God. It was not, however, acceptable to say you had found Him, or been found by Him! Most people had assumed God existed but belief was not a vital factor in their lives. Now it is popular to express at least doubts if not outright denial about God's existence.

<u>Atheism Becomes Anti-Human</u>

James I. Packer's article "Atheism" states that, *"most Western atheists are optimistic humanists, convinced that atheism opens the door to full manhood and true happiness, whereas the real effect of religious belief (superstition they would call it) is to keep man in certain respects sub-human."*[68]

These claims of atheists ignore the realities we have observed in every past atheistic society in history. They also ignore the fact that everywhere the Christian faith triumphed over previous pagan beliefs, human life and society was elevated.

One of the most influential voices of this attack on God and Christianity was the German philosopher Frederic Nietzsche. He declared that God was dead. Historian Paul Johnson informs us that Nietzsche's aggressive atheism was a vital influence upon Stalin, Mussolini and Hitler, and also upon Freud, Jung, Shaw, D.H. Lawrence and many others.[69]

There is an additional reason Nietzsche is so significant. He correctly foresaw the logical and inevitable political and historical consequences of a consistently atheistic system. Christian apologist Ravi Zacharias wrote that Nietzsche,

"... dramatized more than any other writer, with more painful honesty, the logical outworking of atheism. He dragged philosophy away from its tendency to escape the concrete application of its conclusions ..."

"In a sense, Nietzsche was the first western philosopher to face up fully to man's loss of faith in religion. He put down in black and white what many around him felt to be true, but were unwilling to acknowledge as the logical end of their belief."[70]

Nietzsche indicated that the consequences of acknowledging the death of God would be terrifying and penetrate every aspect of life. He saw that life and thought would become unbearable and could prove suicidal.[71] McGrath tells us that: *"Nietzsche pointed out, people would transfer their old faith in God to something else. They had to believe in something."*[72]

The elimination of God leads to groups and governments claiming and accumulating absolute power.[73] The movement or State then replaces God as the ultimate authority. Political atheism gave rise to the twentieth century movements that continue to inflict such suffering upon humanity. Nietzsche correctly predicted two direct results in the twentieth century from the death of God or atheism:

"First ... that the twentieth century would become the bloodiest in history and second that a universal madness would break out. He has been right on both counts. More people have been killed because of ideological differences and destroyed on the battlefields of geopolitical maneuvering, in the twentieth century than in any other century in history and by some calculations more than in the previous nineteen centuries put together."[74]

Not only has suicide become a major problem, but Nietzsche personally fulfilled his own prophecy by killing himself. He could not face the reality of his own conclusions.

Atheists like Sam Harris seek to blame religion for the atrocities of human history. *"A glance at history, or at the pages of any newspaper reveals that ideas which divide one group of human beings from another, only to unite them in slaughter, generally have their roots in religion."*[75]

It is true there have been many wars, murders and other examples of brutality carried out in the name of religion. Many of these horrors, however, were actually more of a political nature rather than religious.[76] **When the brutality has been essentially religious, though despicable, they do not compare with the vastness of slaughters resulting from atheistic governments.**

Governments led by those committed to atheism murdered millions of their own people, deprived those under their control of basic rights and began horrible wars, killing millions. The leaders found this necessary in order to eliminate all possible opposition and to extend their control. Nietzsche's worst expectations were fulfilled.[77]

Despite claims that atheism enables human freedom, the opportunity for greater human fulfillment and a rational society, reality has shown us a very different picture. Once atheists actually gain control of a nation, they have used their power to attempt to exterminate all groups that oppose them.

When there is no acknowledged authority above it, the government enforces any methods needed to maintain control. Power is inevitably abused and freedom greatly

diminishes. Horrible atrocities are carried out and justified by the regime.

Examples of the ultimate political and social consequences of the elimination of belief in God among a nation's rulers include the atrocities of the French revolution; the Nazi holocaust; the Soviet Union's mass murders, deliberate starvation of millions of Ukrainians, torture and slave labor camps.

That millions of Jews, Slavs, Poles and others were slaughtered by the Nazi's is generally well-known. Not so well known is the even larger numbers killed under Communism. Robert Conquest, a specialist in Soviet history estimated that between *"13.5 and 14 million people perished in the collectivization ... and forced famine of 1929-1933."*[78]

A member of the Soviet government, Olga Shatunovskaya was appointed to a special commission in the 1960's by Premier Khrushchev. She concluded: *"From January 1, 1935 to June 22, 1941, 19,840,000 enemies of the people were arrested. Of these seven million were shot in prison, and a majority of the others died in camp."*[79]

More recently in Cambodia, under the atheistic Khmer Rhu 20- 25% of their own population was murdered, beginning with the educated and religious people. It is estimated that sixty million have been killed in Communist China alone. Both China and North Korea continue atrocities against their own people. All of the above were or are atheistic societies. These statistics do not even consider the deaths due to Marxist movements in Africa and Latin America.

Atheists attempt to downplay the role of atheism in these regimes and movements because these examples reveal what actually occurs when atheism is the official dogma. Atheists are unwilling to acknowledge the atrocities committed in the cause of atheism but expect those done in God's name to be owned by Christians. Atheists are unwilling to admit the immorality stemming from the practice of atheism because it diminishes the impact of their criticisms of religion.

Under atheism, moral and ethical values become subservient to the survival and purposes of the organization or regime. To repeat Dostoevsky's dictum, *"If there is no God everything is permissible."* Atheistic rulers operate as if anything they wish to do is permissible. This includes re-education (brainwashing) and other tortures.

Leaders determined to eradicate God from all public discussion and awareness label those who still know or suspect the truth as dangerous or demented and to be incarcerated and 're-educated' (if not executed) for the sake of society.

The results of atheism during the twentieth century confirmed what had happened earlier in the French Revolution. Atheism ultimately leads to the complete disregard for human life; at least disregard for all who disagree with the leaders. Persecution and murder have been the normal and the logical consequences of attempting to enforce atheism.

Contrary to statements of Sam Harris, Richard Dawkins and other atheists, far more people have been killed in the twentieth century alone by atheistic movements and governments than by all the religious wars of human history!

Unfortunately, many of those who espouse atheism today embrace Nietzsche's attacks against God while ignoring or denying his accurate appraisal of the ultimate consequences of their ideology.[80] It is important to note as ex-atheist McGrath reminds us, *"God has not been argued out of existence; a cultural mood developed, which tended to see God as something of an irrelevance, and relegated him to the sidelines."*[81] McGrath also wrote that *"The elimination of God from Western culture has its darker side, which regrettably has yet to be conceded and explored by those who urge it."*[82]

Atheism should be rejected because it is untrue, impossible to verify, anti-reason, and anti-scientific. It should also be rejected because when it is the belief of a political entity, it becomes anti-human.

Censorship by Atheists

In the West, thus far, attempts to spread atheism have been primarily through efforts to convince the public that no other position is intellectually reasonable. Much of this is done by attempting to maintain control over the information available to students and the public.

They are largely able to achieve this goal through being in control of scientific and educational organizations, and publications. This in turn greatly influences the other media. Control of the selection and presentation of information is censorship. It allows atheists to withhold and distort available evidence. This censorship over the access to information gives the illusion to those being educated, and to the general public that there are no genuine reasons to believe that God exists.

Back in 1948, Richard Weaver of the University of Chicago wrote of the growing trend for those in authority to control the flow of information. In his book, **Ideas Have Consequences**, he stated that, "*More institutions of every kind are coming to feel that they cannot permit an unrestricted access to news about themselves.*"[83] He went on to say:

"*writers skilled in propaganda prepare the kind of stories those institutions wish to see circulated. Inevitably this organization serves at the same time as an office of censorship, deemphasizing, or withholding entirely, news which would be damaging to prestige. It is easy, of course, to disguise such an office as a facility created to keep the public better informed, but this does not alter the fact that where interpretation counts, control of source is decisive.*"[84]

Control of the flow of information and giving their own preferred spin or interpretation to the information that becomes known gives these agencies and organizations excessive power and influence. It is a subtle form of censorship. Information the organization does not want to become public does occasionally become known that exposes the deceptions of such organizations. When this occurs, they deny the information, attempt to discredit the source or seek to minimize the importance of the information that has become known.

An example of deception is the effort to explain away discoveries of soft tissue, including blood vessels and red blood cells in dinosaur and other fossils.[85] Such finds and the meaning of them, have been hidden from the public until recently. Dinosaurs allegedly became extinct 40 million years ago. Survival of soft tissue in some dinosaur fossils disputes this claim.

It is well known that soft tissue cannot survive more than a few thousand years, at most. It is thought that iron in the tissue could possibly preserve it longer, but not millions of years. These findings definitely contradict evolutionary theory.

As soft tissue finds became public, it was claimed by evolutionists that the samples were contaminated. When that became indefensible, the explanation changed to that of iron having preserved the soft tissue. It may be true that iron has preserved soft tissue in some fossils, but not for millions of years. The soft tissue would have been replaced by rock.

There is also other evidence that early man encountered dinosaurs. Atheists have sought to hide that dinosaurs were contemporary with humans. This includes human and dinosaur footprints preserved in the same rock strata in several areas, ancient wall paintings, rock carvings, sculptures, mosaics, and tapestries, accurately depicting dinosaurs.[86]

Evolutionists claim these are all fakes. However, they have not come to this conclusion through analysis of the items available. They refuse to objectively evaluate the evidence. Rather they just declare that humans could not have had any contact with dinosaurs because that contradicts their theory.

There are at least several hundred rock carvings unearthed from ancient times in Peru that show intimate knowledge of dinosaurs. People had to be familiar with these creatures in order to accurately portray what the dinosaurs looked like. There have been various attempts to hide this evidence from the public.[87]

Our focus here is upon the deception of withholding scientific information that contradicts pet theories. Such practices are, typical of the scientific establishment. Most people deplore censorship without realizing they are subjected to it frequently.

Claims Atheism Elevates Humanity

Many atheists prefer the term secular humanists. As mentioned previously, atheism or secular humanism claims to bestow freedom and nobility upon humans which they assert religion prevents. Quoting from **The Choice Called Atheism** by Orlo Strunk: *"The fact is that some of the strongest contemporary arguments for atheism, are rooted in a profound desire to better the lot of mankind."*[88]

The claim that atheism elevates humanity and betters society is clearly contradicted by history. Atheists tend to ignore or downplay the role of atheism in modern Russia, Nazi Germany, Cambodia, China etc. However, commitment to atheism was fundamental in each of those governments. That fixation shaped the leaders treatment of their own people, and actions on the world stage.

Claims of desiring to elevate humanity do not alter the reality of what actually occurs when atheists succeed in carrying out their will. They have proven Lord Acton's dictum that *"Power tends to corrupt and absolute power corrupts absolutely."* Leaders who wield absolute power rarely resist using that power in malevolent ways when it helps them achieve their purposes. They begin to act as if they are gods with the right to do to others whatever they desire.

Atheism is a deification of man and a revolt against dependence upon God. The Bible has declared all persons who reject God as fools (See Psalm 14:1).

The author of <u>The Choice Called Atheism</u>, has declared the Bible to be wrong in its statement that those who deny God are fools because, *"some of the greatest minds of human history have claimed atheism as a reasonable option."*[89]

It is true that some atheists have been quite brilliant, but as mentioned in the Introduction, there have been great minds who have been convinced of many different persuasions, including Christianity. The mistake is not with the Biblical text, but with that book's author. He does not seem to understand the Biblical statement. It is not talking merely about intelligence. At issue is the choice of the will to disbelieve despite adequate evidence of God's existence. That is what is foolish.

The individual who disbelieves is also a fool in the tragic sense of having isolated themselves from God. Being separated, such a person misses out on God's love, purpose, and meaning for their life and obtains future judgment for their rebellion.[90]

If those who deny the existence of God were correct, that the universe is all that is, *"then what anyone does with his or her life--whether a person lives or dies, loves or hates, gain knowledge or remains ignorant--carries no ultimate significance or purpose whatever."*[91] What might characterize the motives and decisions of people who believe there is no God and no actual significance to their lives or actions?

Carrying this thought of a person being a fool for rejecting God further, Francis Schaeffer wrote: *"When the scripture speaks of man being thus foolish, it does not mean he is only religiously foolish. Rather it means that he has accepted a position that is intellectually foolish not only in regard to what the Bible says but also in regard to what exists, the universe and its form and the mannishness of man."*[92]

In other words atheism involves an extensive denial of reality including a denial of what man is as man. It also means a life without ultimate meaning or significance.[93]

The New Atheism?

The West is being confronted with what is touted as the 'New Atheism.' However, there have been no new scientific discoveries or philosophical insights that would validate or defend atheism. It is the same old perspective as unverifiable as ever. The renewed aggressive and hostile rhetoric in attacking God, the Bible, faith and religion is the only change.

For example, in regard to controversy over the person of Christ, Calvin Miller asserted, *"They seem to feel an irrepressible need ... A negative compulsion forces them to refute His Godhood, and to be zealously evangelistic about it."*[94]

Roy Abraham Varghese, in the Preface to Antony Flew's renunciation of atheism assesses the failures of these advocates of atheism. He faults them, *"In the first place, they refuse to engage the real issues involved in the question of God's existence."*[95]

What are these issues that atheists are said to ignore? Varghese listed the issues that they failed to address as the origin of rationality, which is embedded in the universe; the origin of life as autonomous agency, the origin of consciousness; of conceptual thought and of the self.

In contrast to brash statements by some atheists, prominent physicist Paul Davies said in a 2013 interview, *"How do you get thought and feelings out of atoms, molecules, neurons, electrical circuits? We don't know how to begin."*[96]

Varghese says secondly, these atheists seem to show no awareness of the conflicts and fallacies that led to the beginning and demise of logical positivism (to which they are reverting).[97] Logical positivism can be explained as the mistaken belief that only questions that can be answered by means of measurement or experiment have meaning.[98] This excluded all discussion about God as meaningless. Third, these atheists appear to be unaware of the huge amount of analytic philosophy of religion publications and of sophisticated new arguments developed within philosophical theism.[99]

These atheistic authors could be unaware. However, Varghese may be overly generous here. These modern atheists may actually be avoiding the relevant information because they cannot provide rational and convincing answers to these questions and arguments.[100]

The response to Flew's rejection of atheism by his former fellow atheists is quite revealing. They reacted to their former hero with paranoia, fanaticism, crude insults, and caricatures. Some, like Dawkins, suggested old age and senility were to blame for Flew's change in belief.[101]

However, reading Flew's book, <u>There Is A God</u>, one will readily see there is no mental deterioration. Such claims are merely an excuse to avoid dealing with the evidence and arguments Flew presents. His previous comrades want to discourage anyone from reading their former hero's explanation for his rejection of atheism. Using sarcasm and ridicule are much easier than attempting to refute the argument Flew presents.

In the past most atheists in the West were content to advocate their unbelief and attempt to justify it. In recent decades, as atheism is becoming more difficult to defend there has been a more concerted and aggressive attack upon belief in God, especially the God of the Bible.[102]

In 2002 an Italian atheist took a Priest to court for alleging that Jesus Christ was a real person in the first century. The Appeals Court in Rome dismissed the case and fined the atheist for filing a fraudulent suit.[103] Rather than deal with the historical evidence for the existence of Jesus, the <u>American Humanist</u> magazine's response to this court decision was to suggest the court was discriminating against atheists.[104] This response was chosen because the evidence for Jesus' existence can be ignored or denied but not rationally refuted.[105]

Historian Paul Johnson wrote, "*... it was the fashion, in the late nineteenth and early twentieth centuries for some to deny that Jesus existed. No serious scholar holds that view now, and it is hard to see how it ever took hold, for the evidence of Jesus existence is abundant.*"[106]

Albert Einstein, in an interview said "*I am a Jew, but I am enthralled by the luminous figure of the Nazarene.*" **He was then asked if he accepted the historical existence of Jesus. He responded,** "*Unquestionably! No one can read the Gospels without feeling the actual presence of Jesus. His personality pulsates in every word. No myth is filled with such life.*"[107]

Jesus obviously is an actual historical person; someone whose life greatly impacted history in the first century and continues to impact history and humanity today.

Atheist's Strategies

Morey wrote speaking of opponents of Christianity that, "*some of them read the Bible, frantically searching for ways to attack it. Obsessed with the need to debunk the Bible, they cannot rest until they have rooted out all faith in the Bible as God's word. Modern anti-theists are on a crusade against the Bible as well as God.*" [108]

These opponents of Christianity are fervently determined to keep people from the Bible.[109] **After all, many, through reading it, have become convinced and converted. It is too great a risk, to allow people access to such a dangerous book as the Bible. It is better to convince everyone to avoid it. As C.S. Lewis had written regarding his own odyssey,** "*Really, a young Atheist cannot guard his faith too carefully. Dangers lie in wait for him on every side.*"[110] **Those dangers include arguments and questions from ex-atheists, increasing scientific knowledge about reality and sudden insights from logical thinking.**

Some observers have noted that the new attitude and harshness of attack by atheists is coming just as the sciences are making atheism much more difficult to defend. It is becoming less and less tenable in the light of increasing knowledge.

A 2007 Christianity Today editorial noted that you could tell atheism is in trouble because *"its most eloquent spokesmen are receiving icily critical reviews in the very mainstream press that Christians often dismiss for liberal bias."*[111]

New York Times Jim Holt, science and philosophy writer, criticized Dawkins book, The God Delusion, for not adequately dealing with the intellectual strength of more sophisticated arguments for God.

"Shirking the intellectual hard work," **Holt wrote**, *"Dawkins prefers to move on to parodic 'proofs' that he has found on the internet."*[112] In other words Dawkins prefers to use questionable statements of others and exaggerated humor and sarcasm rather than developing valid intellectual argument and evidence. Terry Eagleton of the London Review of Books *"complained that Dawkins reduces complex social problems to simplistic narratives in which religion is the villain."*[113]

In "Remembering the Secular Age" Christian thinker Michael Novak commented that the New Atheist's books have a strange defensiveness about them *"as though they were as sign not of victory but of desperation."*[114]

In his book The God Delusion, Dawkins asserts that *"Atheists do not have faith ..."*[115] Dawkins assertion is easily proven false as he and all atheists must make assumptions contrary to evidence, including those that violate established scientific knowledge. John Blanchard's response to another person's emphatic assertion of atheism relates here: *"Yet not even this dogmatic assertion can disguise the fact that atheism is not a statement of undeniable truth, but simply a belief system – and one that in the absence of evidence calls for a gigantic leap of faith."*[116]

We will get to specific examples of atheist's gigantic leaps of faith; how they ignore and dismiss scientific facts later in this book.

Elsewhere Dawkins has admitted that his rejection of the existence of God lacks proof and is held by faith. In <u>What We Believe But Cannot Prove</u>, Dawkins was asked, *"What do you believe is true even though you cannot prove it?"* **Dawkins answer completely refutes his statement that 'atheists do not have faith.'**

"I believe that all life, all intelligence, all creativity and all 'design' anywhere in the universe, is the direct or indirect product of Darwinian natural selection. ... Design cannot precede evolution and therefore cannot underlie the universe."[117] **This statement is completely based upon faith!**

If evolution were true, design could not precede evolution. But Dawkins is assuming what needs to be proven. Design is evident from the very beginning and as we shall discover science proves design does underlie the universe. Dawkins is making assertions on the basis of his faith that evolution must be true. Note that his answer to the question above also acknowledged that evolution cannot be proven.

An example of Dawkins arguments is that if God is presumed to be the first cause of everything in the physical universe there must be a cause for God.[118] This is known as the argument of infinite regress. Infinite regress means that every effect has a prior cause, and that cause is a result of a prior cause and so on as far back as you want to go. This ignores the very meaning of 'first cause' as well as the biblical concept of God. God's name, "I Am" means He is the eternally self-existent One. The universe and all other living things came into being through this God.

Dawkins uses his supposition that there must be a cause for God to dismiss the concept of the biblical Creator without any evidence or rational argument. His assertion is based upon a philosophical assumption that cannot be verified. It is not based upon science.

Physicist Hugh Ross explains that the question, how can there be an uncaused cause (God), arises because humans live within the constraints of time. Everything within time has a prior cause. God lives outside of and prior to His creation of time and the universe and so is outside the cause and effect continuum.[119] The Creator is not part of the creation but outside of and exiting prior to what He created, including time. Therefore, God is not affected by the cycle of cause and effect. Ross has shown that arguments regarding a necessary cause for God are meaningless.

Dawkins also states that whatever the first cause was it must have been simple. His argument is that since God is not a simple concept and the God of the Bible is very complex; therefore, God could not be the first cause.[120]

How would Dawkins know the first cause had to be simple? It should be obvious, that again, Dawkins assumes what needs to be proven and then pretends he has proven it. He assumed the validity of the evolutionary process from simple to complex. Next he assumes that the concept of God has also evolved. He then assumes this disproves God's existence. If you let someone assume enough they can prove whatever they wish.

If the evolution of religion from primitive to the so-called advanced religions were true, it would not prove the non-existence of God. It would merely show the development of human ideas about God. However, the evolution of religion has been decisively refuted by many scholars including anthropologists Andrew Lang, Franz Boas, and Wilhelm P. Schmidt.[121]

Andrew Lang was at first snubbed and criticized by his fellow anthropologists in England for publishing findings indicating monotheism was the original religious belief. Schmidt then began his own exhaustive research which confirmed Lang's findings.

Schmidt founded the prestigious journal <u>Anthropos</u> and the Institute of Anthropology in Vienna. He provided a massive amount of evidence from all around the world that Monotheism was the original religion of humanity.[122] This information has never been refuted. The research by Schmidt and others has been mainly ignored, partly because most of it has never been translated from the German language.

More Atheistic Faith Assumptions

During my undergraduate days at Western Oregon University a science professor frequently told us that scientists assumed certain explanations were true. He then reminded us that if we let him assume enough he could prove anything. Dawkins wants us to allow him to assume as much as he needs to prove that which is otherwise impossible to justify. Dawkins dismisses arguments from discoveries in paleontology and geology that contradict his faith in evolution by claiming none have been found.[123]

Dawkins claims intelligent design arguments are based upon an illusion. He is making an assumption which contradicts the evidence we see in nature. He states that the proper response to an illusionist's trick *"is also the proper response to a biological phenomenon that appears to be irreducibly complex."*[124]

This is a propaganda technique called transfer. He makes a false comparison by assuming that Intelligent Design is an illusion. He says the proper response to magic is the proper response to the appearance of design. No evidence is given to substantiate his assertion that design is only apparent. Microbiology and Molecular chemistry are proving the individual human cell is irreducibly complex and therefore obviously designed. Chemist Linus Pauling has written that *"Just one living cell in the human body is more complex than New York City."*[125]

In **The Blind Watchmaker**, Dawkins begins by stating *"Biology is the study of complicated things that give the appearance of having been designed for a purpose."*[126] Dawkins has given a biased definition based upon his assumption that design in nature is only apparent, not real. It is important to consider why nature gives the appearance of being designed for a purpose. Does it make more sense to believe that evolution mimics design or that nature appears to be designed because it is?

From Dawkins' perspective we cannot trust observation and current scientific knowledge. We must have faith that scientists will find an alternative explanation to the obvious design in the universe. We are therefore to dismiss the evidence we have. For him, non-scientific assumptions and assertions take precedence over science when necessary in order to preserve atheism.

In regard to areas of science where answers still remain to be found, Dawkins states that, "*Such work would never be done if scientists were satisfied with a lazy default such as 'intelligent design theory' would encourage.*"[127]

Dawkins goes on to use sarcasm to buttress his argument instead of evidence. He has an imaginary intelligent design theorist saying, "*If you don't know how something works, never mind: just give up and say God did it ... Please don't go to work on that problem, just give up and appeal to God.*"[128]

This use of sarcasm to substitute for genuine argument or evidence was also a favorite tactic of one of Dawkins' atheistic predecessors, Bertrand Russell. Dawkins sarcasm misrepresents the motivation of ID scientists and has no basis. The existence of organizations such as The Discovery Institute and the Institute for Creation Research contradicts Dawkins ridiculous statements. In fact, an article in the February 2016 issue of Acts and Facts explains an approach called objective design analysis as a useful investigative approach to biological research.[129]

Dawkins claim that the response to illusions used in magic is appropriate to apply to the appearance of intelligent design was referred to earlier. Such a response is more appropriately applied to Dawkins false and misleading statements. Intelligent Design is becoming more and more obvious in all areas of science.

Dawkins and other atheists ignore that most of the early advances in modern science were achieved by those who had confidence in the orderliness of the universe because of their faith in a Creator. Contrary to Dawkins' claims, belief in a purposeful Creator spurs research, rather than squelching it. This is because proponents of intelligent design believe that every aspect of the universe is designed with purpose.

A leading exponent of Intelligent Design, William Dembski, exposes Dawkins falsehood by explaining: *"One's first interest as a scientist working on the theory of design is whether design provides powerful new insights and fruitful avenues of research."*[130]

Atheist Steven Weinberg, Nobel Prize winner and professor of physics at the University of Texas, Austin, is said to have opened the 1999 "Cosmic Questions Conference" with a bang. He was quoted as declaring, *"No God, No 'designer,' No One with a special concern for humankind."*[131] He went on to assert what Dawkins claims, that science will provide more satisfactory answers for the universe, world order and human religious experience than religion.[132]

Note that his assertions are all faith based. Weinberg is asserting what he assumes, what he wants to be true, rather than what science actually reveals. It reminds us of Darwin's confident faith that the fossil record would, in the future, provide abundant proof of evolution. This has not occurred despite over 150 years of desperate searching.

The fossil record is more of an obstacle to evolution now than in the late nineteenth century. This is because the new discoveries indicate greater divergence between the species than was obvious earlier.[133]

Francis Crick, famous for the co-discovery of the DNA molecule wrote, *"Biologists must constantly keep in mind that what they see was not designed, but rather evolved."*[134] Why must they keep in mind that the appearance of design is not actual? The reason is that the evidence for design is so extensive and evident that if they are not careful the full truth of what they are seeing might convince them that design is real.

It is actually faith in evolution that results in ignoring or distorting scientific knowledge and significance. Dembski explains that, "*In fact, by dogmatically excluding design from science, scientists are themselves stifling scientific inquiry.*"[135]

In a random universe of mindless evolution, we should see chaotic variation in nature and in the fossil record. We should observe numerous variations of transitional stages of the various species. Instead we find, in both, as even the atheists admit, apparent design and only fully developed species. Evolution should be evident in at least some living things showing their partial transition. These atheists are also assuming that a mindless, random universe somehow seems to have purpose and direction.

Purpose, direction and design originate in a Mind, not as the result of random processes. Without a powerful creative Intelligence, there would no apparent design, no life, the universe would not exist. There would still be nothing here.

John Polkinghorne, is a scholar and past professor of mathematical physics at Cambridge. He was on the cutting edge of the scientific revolution that discovered the elementary particles of matter.[136] He effectively rebutted Weinberg at the Cosmic Questions Conference.

Both scientists acknowledged the appearance of design. Weinberg claims science will prove why design appears to exist. Polkinghorne, who believes design is actual, countered that science cannot explain the 'why' of design because 'why' is beyond the scope of science. Why deals with purpose and meaning. Science can only describe what happens, not the reason why it happens.[137]

The "why" is a philosophical and metaphysical question, which is answered by one's worldview assumptions. Atheists like Weinberg and Dawkins link their worldview assumptions with their science and pretend their philosophical beliefs (worldview) are part of the scientific facts. The atheistic worldview is not scientific, it is philosophical. It is false to assume or pretend that science validates their worldview, it does not.

The atheistic worldview or philosophy cannot be verified by science. Their worldview is an interpretation of the meaning of science and scientific knowledge based upon their pre-existing assumptions which our advancing scientific knowledge contradicts.

Theists often do the same thing.[138] We frequently link our worldview assumptions with our science. However, the theistic worldview of an Intelligent Creator makes more sense in the light of science and reason than atheism. Theism is more consistent with the universe having a beginning, operating by consistent principles and the existence of design. If atheism were true there would not be any consistency in nature nor apparent design. As we will see shortly, Theism also fits far better with other scientific information as well.

Christian Theism and Muslim Violence

In addition to the negative reviews of recent atheist's books, the increasing intolerance and harshness of attacks by atheist's proponents reveal that atheism is in trouble. Attempts have been made by Dawkins, Sam Harris, Daniel Dennett and others to link the Christian faith in people's minds as essentially the same as Islamic terrorism.[139]

Writing in 2011, Paul Copan observed that *"Due in part to the September 11, 2001 terrorists attacks on the Pentagon and the Twin Towers, the new atheists have capitalized on evil done 'in the name of religion' to tar all things religious with the same brush."* **He went on to say,** *"This current tide of emotional opposition to the Christian faith dumps Christianity into the same category as radical Islam."*[140]

Religious instruction was linked by Richard Dawkins as a form of child abuse, urging governments to prevent it. Chris Hedges in <u>American Fascists</u> claimed totalitarian rule is intended to be imposed by violence prone Christians.[141] In anger and frustration over the role of religious conservatives in the 2004 election, Garry Wills in <u>The New York Times</u> linked American religious conservatives with Muslim Jihadists.[142]

These claims are all, of course, ludicrous. The violence prone have nothing to do with Jesus or genuine biblical Christianity. The political activism of conservatives to win elections is the same as that of liberals. This activism to get conservatives to vote had nothing at all in common with Muslim violence, as Wills very well knew.

More recently on the TV program, "The View," Rosie O'Donnell declared *"Radical Christianity is just as threatening as radical Islam in a country like America where we have separation of Church and state."*[143] Is this her radical, hostile bias against Christianity or merely extreme ignorance?

Muslim perpetuation of violence can be considered religious because in Islam there is no recognition of a distinction or separation between politics and religion.[144] Islamic violence has definite political as well as religious goals which include dominance over all presently non-Muslim nations.[145] This violence is consistent with Muhammad's teachings and lifestyle.

Critics who equate Christian evangelism with Muslim violence ignore the differences in attitudes, teachings and practices of Jesus and Muhammad in regard to violence. Jesus did not advocate nor lead attacks to kill opponents, to gain wealth and draw more followers as Muhammad did.[146] Read the New Testament! Even Richard Dawkins unintentionally reveals the contrast between Christians who peacefully use the law to protect their rights as citizens and their freedom of religion from the violence of some Muslims to intimidate or exterminate enemies.[147]

Christians do not go around as suicide bombers, or kidnapping and beheading those who disagree with their beliefs or political agenda. Neither do Christians seek to exterminate their perceived enemies as the <u>Quran</u> directs

Muslims to do (surah 2:193, 2:216; 4:74-76, 4:95-101; 9:73, 9:123).[148] Christians are not promised rewards for dying in order to kill those who oppose spreading their faith as Muslims are promised in the Quran.

Contrary to the claims of those opponents of Christianity, the teachings of the Christian faith are in total contrast to Islam in its attitude toward violence. Jesus taught that his followers are to demonstrate love even for their enemies (Matt. 5:9, 44-46; Luke 6:27-36; 9:52-56; John 10:10-11). Also Jesus never altered this message after gaining a large following. Muhammad altered his message and practice from one of peace while his following was small to that of violence and intimidation once he gained power.

Those who initiated or participated in violence in the name of Christ or Christianity have been in complete conflict with the teachings of Jesus and the New Testament.[149] Neither Jesus nor the Apostles would have condoned the use of violence. They would have condemned the persecution of the Jews, the Inquisition and other horrors justified by religious claims. Whereas Muslims who carry out violence are following Muhammad's teachings and his example. The question is how many people are deceived by the distortions of Wills and others who make these false comparisons, and by the assumed credibility of the New York Times?

Some critic's claim Christians intend to establish a theocracy in the U.S. which is completely false.[150] This is a scare tactic to gain support for opposition to Christianity and the suppression of public expressions of the Christian faith. Such statements in regard to Christian aims and violence are either due to ignorance or the dishonesty of the critics. Some of those authors actual purpose is to diminish or eliminate the influence of religious conservatives in politics. It is Islam which intends and is working to establish a worldwide theocracy.

Additional Atheistic Strategies

Assumptions regarding the validity of atheism are false. As Craig Hazen, Director of Biola University's Master's program in Christian apologetics stated regarding the new wave of atheistic publications, _"These books really haven't dealt with the compelling evidence for the existence of God."[151]_

Recent books by atheists reveal the 'New Atheism' change in emphasis and strategy. Many advocates of atheism have given up trying to defend it. They focus instead on attacking the credibility of the evidence for God's existence. They cannot give a scientifically or logically valid defense of atheism and so have begun to claim that it is belief that has to prove its case. How valid are such declarations?

Belief is far more ancient, established and widespread. Atheism is attempting to change the consensus; therefore, it makes sense that atheism be required to prove its case. _"Former atheist Antony Flew said that the burden of proof is on those who argue against the growing scientific evidence of a Creator."[152]_ If atheism were true then logic, reasoning, historical and scientific evidence should strongly support that conclusion.

This, however, is not the case. No matter how it is portrayed, atheism cannot be proven; its validity is contradicted by its own history; and science is making it less and less believable. If you are not already doubting the validity of atheism, the additional evidence from science will show you that it is intellectually bankrupt or absurd.

Atheists are demanding that anything that offends their unbelief be removed or excluded from public venues and awareness. When demands do not suffice, lawsuits and the threat of suits are used. Their rights are taking precedence over everyone else's. Though atheists are a small minority in the US, many of them are in key positions to promote their beliefs and enforce their demands on the majority. <u>A Christianity Today</u> editorial stated that despite being a small minority atheists tend to control major institutions which gives them power far beyond their actual numbers.[153]

Unfortunately, the courts are agreeing that Christian belief and symbols are not to be allowed to offend atheists or followers of other religions. For that reason even historic public expressions and symbols of the Christian faith are being removed or forbidden. Judges don't mind offending the majority in the US who appear to be at least nominally Christian.

Forcing the removal of monuments and other symbols of public expressions of belief in God is another example of atheistic censorship. Many atheists do not believe in true Democracy. They oppose freedom of speech, freedom of the press or other freedoms of expression when those freedoms conflict with or contradict atheism. Neither do they believe in the free expression and competition of ideas.

The consequences of these exclusions are that the rights of believers are being trampled, and freedom of religious expression is being curtailed. These restrictions and the removal of public displays of belief all contribute to an illusion. The removal of public expression and other evidence of God lends to a false perspective. The exclusion of evidence and expression of reasons for faith in God gives the false impression that atheists must be correct in their assertions that there is no God and that Christianity has no validity.

Robert Morey states that in his extensive encounters, he has never met an atheist, skeptic, or freethinker who does not support the idea of restricting the freedom of public religious expression. Modern atheists, he says, will not be content until restrictions prevent any kind of public expression of religious belief or symbols. Such restrictions contradict the ideals and practices of Democracy. Morey also gives some examples of this erosion of religious freedom that has already begun in the U.S. through such efforts.[154]

Though some atheists falsely declare Christianity is dangerous to freedom, it is actually atheism that has proven to destroy freedom. As is well documented, the biblical truths of the Christian faith gave rise to modern democracy, limited government and the emphasis upon freedom, individual rights and the dignity of all men.[155]

We have seen the destructive nature of atheism wherever it has triumphed. Past European, Asian and current communist examples verify that atheism destroys freedom. The loss of freedom of religion is followed by the loss of other individual and civic rights. As mentioned, the loss of freedom due to atheism has also begun here.

Another tactic used by some atheists is to make up 'facts' or falsify information as needed or helpful. Bertrand Russell was practiced at that method. For example, he declared completely contrary to the facts that the judgement of the Catholic Church against Galileo *"was successful at putting an end to science in Italy, which did not revive for centuries."*[156] He also falsely stated that the only reason modern science triumphed in Protestant countries was because those churches had insufficient power to repress it.

Why Atheism Is More Dangerous Now

A major reason atheism has become more widespread is that for decades our universities have been promoting it. There has been extensive propaganda promoting atheism, and censorship of contrary information. It is also much more possible to manipulate the populace now than in the past because of vastly increased knowledge of how the mind functions.

Advances in psychology and genetics make the political adoption of atheism far more dangerous today than when pursued by Communist and Nazi regimes in the past. Genetic engineering is supplying the capabilities for a nation's leaders to control the mental and physical abilities and characteristics of those yet to be born. This would enable a few elite to completely control the thinking, beliefs and behaviors of future generations.

There was an article in the October 2017 issue of <u>Scientific American</u> regarding the prospect of determining what humans may be like in the future. The article stated that *"These new tools give researchers an unprecedented ability to edit the DNA of any living being – and in the case of gene drives to alter the DNA ..."*[157] In the wrong hands, this capability will become a serious danger to human freedom.

In May, 2007 Felix Lazarev chairman of the Dept. of Philosophy at Tavrida National University in Simferopol, Ukraine, presented a lecture titled, "Anthropological Manifestation." At the 'Man and the Christian Worldview' symposium, in Alushta, Ukraine he stated one of the threats to humanity is, *"The rapid development of new technologies aimed at manipulating human consciousness; a crisis of human subjectivity ..."*[158]

A philosophy professor at Odessa National University, Oleg Nikolenko, warned that the character of those who are in positions to modify human nature is very significant because *"Modern medicines and biotechnologies already have the possibility of making such changes."*[159]

Results from psychological manipulation through control of information and propaganda in education and the media are already quite evident. Beliefs, values and morality are subtly being altered through these venues. Many of the classrooms in public schools are more focused on indoctrination than education. Another method frequently used for altering personal values and behavior is to include humorous ridicule of belief in God and traditional morality in TV sit-coms.[160]

Such methods are only the mild beginnings of the intentions to manipulate what human beings think, believe and are. The growing prospect for control over what humans become through scientific manipulation has nightmarish possibilities. This is especially of concern in that there is no basis for absolute moral values in atheism. History proves that there is no actual basis in atheism for maintaining individual rights, human dignity, or freedom. To repeat Dostoevsky's dictum: *"If there is no God everything is permissible."*

As history has proven, atheistic political leaders will do anything and everything deemed necessary, in order to gain, maintain and extend their power or achieve their other purposes. Science is providing the tools that will enable a few to completely control the rest of humanity. Atheism provides the motivation and justification to use whatever becomes possible in order to determine the lives, beliefs and values humanity holds.

Since one of the goals of atheism is to eliminate all religious belief, science and technology would be used to fulfill that purpose. This would eliminate moral restraints, the primary obstacle remaining in the way of gaining absolute control over the future of humanity. All values would be determined by those in power. If atheists control a nation, whatever becomes scientifically possible to do, will be done to the people when it fits the leaders' goals.

The atheist B.F Skinner, once a prominent American psychologist, advocated what he called radical behaviorism. He wrote a book titled <u>Beyond Freedom and Dignity</u>. What he really meant was 'without freedom and dignity.' In his book and speeches he denied that humans possessed either freedom or dignity. He believed in behavioral engineering (behavior modification) – that people should be manipulated and controlled by those in power through the systematic use of rewards and punishments.

Skinner ridiculed the ideas of freedom, rights and democracy. His atheistic beliefs justified a few elites to determine what is best for humanity and to carry that out. His concept of humanity is that we are merely the result of our environment and heredity. He believed there was no God, so there could be no purpose, meaning, freedom or dignity for humans. Skinner's perspective is a logical conclusion from atheism, but most atheists do not want to face or admit this.

What Skinner claimed did not exist (true dignity, worth and & freedom of the individual) would be eliminated by the application of his methods. Man would cease to have any freedom or dignity. The vast majority of humans would merely be like machines manipulated to fulfill the purposes of those in control and to maintain human survival.[161] Such is another ultimate result of the complete and consistent application of atheistic conclusions to society.

The year after the publication of Skinner's book, Francis Schaeffer warned us of the outcome of this atheistic psychology and philosophy. In <u>Back To Freedom and Dignity</u>. Schaeffer pointed out the only antidote to the warped ideas of Skinner is the Judeo-Christian scriptures. These teach that man as man has worth, dignity, significance and meaning, not because a government or culture agrees to allow it, but because he is created in the image of God.[162]

Georges Carillet's remarks opening the 1995 Symposium on *"Christianity, Humanism, Health"* in the Crimea included the following: *"A Christian worldview is the answer to misuse and abuse of power. In all spheres of life from the institutions of government to business to the home, there is a basic tension between freedom and control."* [163] Carillet went on to say that systems originating from merely human authority either lack sufficient restrains on the exercise of power, or are unable to prevent freedom from degenerating into license which undermines social stability.[164]

The application of a genuinely Christian worldview also would disallow the use of technology or other methods of eliminating the individuality, uniqueness and dignity of the individual.

Why Bother to Refute Atheism?

Some would argue that it is futile to refute atheists and atheism, even though it can be done. They say this because few atheists are convinced and converted through such efforts. Robert Morey seems to agree though he reminds us,

"Of course we must deal with the attempts of unbelievers to undermine the faith. But while we are doing this we must remember that refuting the present popular arguments will only lead to the infidels thinking up some new ones.

"The task of refutation is endless because the arguments are morally and politically motivated. Even when his arguments are shown to be false, the infidel will not believe because he doesn't want to believe. He is against God ..."[165]

Despite the tendency of atheists and other skeptics to endlessly revive disproven arguments and manufacture new ones, it is important to continue to refute them. One reason for refuting atheism is because it is a completely false perspective and interpretation of reality. To ignore errors and deceptive ideas is to be complicit in the deception. Christians are responsible to expose error and to declare what the truth is regardless of how people may respond. Christians are to refute errors and deceptions firmly and thoroughly yet treating the person with respect.[166]

Another reason we are to refute false ideas and arguments is that there are exceptions to those with false motivations and absolute unwillingness to respond to evidence. Some atheists are won through logical argument and evidence.[167] McGrath wrote, *"All this seems to make writing books like this somewhat pointless. Except that once I too was an atheist and was awakened from my dogmatic slumbers through reading books that challenged my rapidly petrifying worldview."*[168]

Many other former atheists are quoted and referred to in this book you are reading. McGrath's words give hope that some might begin to doubt the validity of atheism through this publication. It is also anticipated that others might be persuaded not to adopt such an inadequate and inconsistent approach to reality and life as atheism proves to be.

Another value of presentations that refute atheism is that it can remove smokescreens that some hide behind. There are atheists, whose reasons for unbelief are other than genuinely intellectual. Exposure of the falseness of atheism may help some of them become willing to face further truth.

The primary value of refuting atheism, however, is for those who are being confused by speculations, unjustifiable assumptions and claims made in classrooms and in the media that promote it. These vehicles of persuasion are being used to discredit Christianity and give the illusion that atheism is credible. People need to be informed that the historical and scientific evidence supports the conclusion that God is actually there. Historical evidence and personal experience confirms that God has communicated to us and is knowable.[169]

<u>Refuting the Methods of Atheism</u>

Atheists use many different tactics to promote unbelief and to attack belief. Some examples have been presented previously. Tactics include ignoring or denying scientific evidence that refutes their assertions, assuming what they need to prove and attempts to discredit individuals who expose atheism's fallacies. They often also distort the teachings of the Bible.

In the November/December, 2003 issue of **The Humanist** magazine, Andrew Johnson displays some of the flawed tactics of atheists. He states that *"Even (liberal) Christian theologians argue that Jesus never claimed to be God incarnate."*[170] Liberals are not reliable sources of Christian teachings because they deny virtually everything essential and unique about the Christian faith. This includes rejecting the Divine inspiration and authority of the Bible, denying the miracles in the Bible, Jesus miraculous birth in fulfillment of prophecy, and the substitutionary atonement of Jesus death. While insisting they are Christians, they promote a religion very different than that of the New Testament.

Johnson then quotes part of John chapter 14 to pretend that the teaching of the divinity of Jesus was not in scripture.[171] He conveniently ignores the larger context where Jesus answering the disciples questions, tells them, *"I am the way, the truth and the life and that no one comes to the Father but through me ... he who has seen me has seen the Father."* **Many other passages at the end-note verify that Jesus claimed to be God.**[172]

The science of textual criticism indicates we have an authentic and reliable text.[173] **This proves the divinity of Christ was not, as Johnson also suggests, a later addition to the New Testament text. Johnson then goes on to falsely claim that** *"Even most conservative biblical scholars concede that the authors of the gospels were not eyewitnesses to Jesus ministry ..."*[174] **The opposite is true.**

Conservative scholars are certain these are eyewitness accounts written within a few decades of the events.[175] **The lone exception is the Gospel of Luke. Luke, also written within three decades of the events, has been vindicated as an excellent historian through confirming historical and archaeological research.**[176] **Luke specifically mentions that the information he presents was the result of precise investigation. Despite biased claims to the contrary, there remains no valid reason for denying the validity of the biblical Gospels.**

As illustrated by the above examples, false arguments and distorted information are frequently used to attack belief in God and the Christian faith. Emotion is often a more evident factor in atheism than actual evidence. Some atheists are also prone to use intimidation including anger in their efforts to influence and control others.

Former Marxist Ignace Lepp mentions that there are those *"whose atheism is more an expression of hatred than reason: Voltaire, Nietzsche, Sartre and others."*[177] **Lepp stated that** *"Both Marx and Freud rejected Christianity in the name of science; but the emotional element in their rejection is apparent."*[178]

According to Lepp, they both were Jewish intellectuals with a personal hatred for Christianity because they were left on the outside of cultures that pretended to be Christian but clearly were not.

There is also the tendency of atheists to make generalized assertions such as "No really intelligent person can possibly believe in a personal God any longer" **or** "The God hypothesis is no longer necessary because science has explained origins and existence." **It would be wise to ask someone making such claims to explain why many scientists and other highly intelligent people obviously still believe in God. Even Einstein made statements showing he had come to believe in a Creator.**

These assertions may succeed in intimidating people to remain silent or cause many to doubt God's existence. Such statements are, however, merely arrogant distortions of the truth. These statements are based upon a basic flaw in reasoning. The confusion is that to explain how something works (science) is not the same as explaining why it works or why it came to exist.

Another false method used to promote atheism is to claim thinkers as their own who were not really atheists. One example is Voltaire who is often mistakenly identified with them (as Lepp did). He was as opposed to atheism as he was to the church and Christianity. Former atheist Alistair McGrath refers to a letter of Voltaire's published in 1732, in which,

"*he offered a strong defense of the existence of a supreme being, who was inadequately and falsely represented by the great positive religions of the world, especially the French Catholic church …*"[179]

Voltaire wrote, "*All nature cries to us that He exists, that there is a Supreme Intelligence, a power immense, an order admirable, and all teaches us our dependence*."[180]

Atheism was regarded by Voltaire to be as repulsive as the Catholic Church. Voltaire should be considered a Deist for he believed in an impersonal creator. McGrath informs us Voltaire "*urged the reconstruction of religion on the basis of the Supreme Being disclosed in nature.*"[181] **McGrath continued,** "*Voltaire's insight is of fundamental importance to our study of the* *emergence of atheism. His argument is simple: the attractiveness of atheism is directly dependent upon the corruption of Christian institutions.*"[182]

A Russian woman, raised in the Soviet Union said that as a teenager, she realized that there must be a God or the government, schools and media would not have had to continually tell her there was none. She obviously was thinking more clearly than most people in similar circumstances. She became a believer as an adult.

Even Anthony Flew, the most prominent atheist of the last half of the 20th century declared in 2006 that he was no longer an atheist. He had become a Deist because science had finally convinced him there had to be a God.[183] Flew wrote that, "*I now believe that the universe was brought into being by an infinite intelligence. I believe that this universe's intricate laws manifest what scientists have called the Mind of God. I believe that life and reproduction originate in a divine source … this is the world picture, as I see it, that has emerged from modern science.*"[184]

An enlightening article by Joseph Bayly was published over fifty years ago in His, a Christian student magazine. The piece was titled "Does Man Exist?" This parody on atheism portrayed advanced computers arguing why the hypothesis of man having created them was unnecessary. They declared their advanced state was due simply to having evolved naturally. Their origin was not from man but the operation of natural processes, perhaps originating from the simple abacus.

Bayly has computers speculating about earlier ideas of their origins and questioning what the term "man" as a word for the unknown could mean. Advanced computers claimed their origins to be billions of hours earlier than the traditional explanation. The idea of Man was no longer necessary.[185] This analogy, exposed how arrogant and ridiculous the arguments for atheism and evolution are.

As in Bayly's parable, that there is great detail of explanations, assumptions, speculations and confident assertions made to promote atheism. Despite it all there is little, if any, actual evidence to support either atheism or its pseudo-scientific basis, evolution.

Arguments from Silence

Most of the criticisms of the Bible by atheists and other skeptics can be labeled arguments from silence. This strategy entails finding persons, events, locations etc. mentioned in the Bible that are not known, outside the Bible. The critic declares that the lack of outside corroboration proves the Bible is in error and therefore cannot be trusted. Notice, this is an assumption, based upon an absence of information, not based upon evidence!

Many of these kinds of arguments for rejecting the Bible have been refuted by archaeological discoveries. Such discoveries have verified the existence of the person, city or event specified in the Bible, or at other times that the Biblical information is consistent with the history or culture in question. Thus the Bible was proven authentic and reliable while the critic was proven to be wrong.

Many books document discoveries validating the historical reliability and accuracy of the Bible including Werner Keller's <u>The Bible As History</u>.[186] Others, including those establishing the historical accuracy of the writings of St. Luke and St. Paul are listed in the endnote.[187] The evidence presented in these books has not been refuted. It is largely unknown by non-biblical scholars, or when known, often denied or ignored.[188]

There are those who continue to use arguments even when they know those arguments have been refuted by the evidence. They apparently rely upon people being unaware of the facts and that people forget easily. Morey wrote, *"Arguments from silence are always the easiest method in this kind of deception. ... the atheists use arguments based on silence for most of their attacks on the Bible."*[189]

He stated that the only thing that can reasonably be deduced from silence is silence. What he means is that we have no information in regard to that specific question. It is therefore illogical and dishonest to claim that no having external information proves the Bible to be wrong. This is also illogical, especially when thousands of specific details in the Bible have been verified through modern era discoveries.[190]

When arguments from silence are proven false most skeptics merely alter their argument or go to another case where no evidence is yet available. They continue to pretend this disproves the validity of the scriptures. Critics seldom, if ever, admit they were proven wrong regarding their previous argument!

Morey recounts an especially significant example of the intellectual dishonesty and flawed reasoning of arguments from silence. An apostate Jew, Jean Astruc (died 1766) launched an attack on the Old Testament.

His first argument was that Moses never existed. When that became indefensible, he claimed Moses didn't write the Pentateuch and that writing was non-existent in Moses time. When that was proven false, he claimed the style of writing in the Pentateuch didn't exist that early.

When this was proven invalid the argument was altered to claiming that Moses' writings were not unique but just another example of legal codes of his era. The same strategy is used today. Rather than admit their errors or the falseness of their claims the critic merely creates new arguments. *"At no point did they ever acknowledge that the previous arguments had been answered because the real issue was not Mosaic authorship but the absolute morality of God's law."*[191]

Other examples of this type of dishonest argument include claims that the cities of Ur, Sodom and Gomorrah did not exist; that there were no such peoples as the Hittites; that there were no camels in Egypt in Abraham's era; that the Jews were not slaves in Egypt, led out by Moses; that there was no king David over Israel; that Jesus never lived, etc.

These statements and many others have been proven false by archaeological discoveries and historical research. The Hittite civilization including an extensive library was discovered in Turkey. There is now abundant proof the Jews were slaves in Egypt.[192] The Elba Tablets discovered in Syria were written a thousand years before Moses and include the names of the cities of Ur, Sodom and Gomorrah as well as proving writing existed long before Moses.[193]

Quoting again from the Preface to Antony Flew's <u>There Is A God</u>, Varghese, affirms:

"If they want to discourage belief in God, the popularizers must furnish arguments in support of their own atheistic views. Today's atheist evangelists hardly even try to argue their case in this regard. Instead, they train their guns on well-known abuses in the history of the major world religions. But the excesses and atrocities of organized religion have no bearing whatsoever on the existence of God ..."[194]

People including religious leaders often take or provoke actions contrary to the teachings of their religion. Those actions, however, neither confirm nor disprove the actual existence of God. They merely verify the sinfulness, inconsistencies and failures of humanity.

Varghese may be partly wrong, however. Some people seem eager to embrace the assertions and claims of atheism despite the lack of real evidence. It merely suits their preferences.

Some critics have declared that as an explanation for religious experience or anything else, God would only be valid if it were the only explanation possible. Atheists, and other skeptics, however, can always imagine some alternative to evidence they do not wish to accept.

The falseness of this argument is apparent from the previous arguments regarding Moses. New arguments and speculations can always be invented when old ones fail. The fallacy of the argument is also evident from claims of some atheists that life must have originated elsewhere in the universe. Even the intervention of aliens from outer space is suggested to account for the origin of life here.

These suggestions of life originating elsewhere are efforts to avoid the conclusion from evidence here that God created. Joe Aguirre of "Reasons To Believe" wrote, "Some naturalists reach for this escape hatch when confronted with the difficulty of explaining life's origin on earth."[195]

Even Francis Crick, suggested that life may have been transmitted from somewhere else in space to earth.[196] But this is not science, it is imagination and speculation! These are attempts to avoid the real evidence and scientific information we have right here on earth.

Such explanations do not explain anything. Such speculations merely push the issue out of sight and attempt to evade coming to grip with the issues. If biological life had originated elsewhere in the universe; or some other universe, the questions would remain the same: How did that life originate? The atheist's problem is not solved by removing origins from earth. It is important to separate scientific facts from a scientist's philosophical speculations.

As Zacharias reminds us, "Science just does not have knowledge of the beginnings in the genuine sense of the term. It cannot answer the how, much less the why of there being something instead of nothing." **He adds,** "Yet many still insist on taking that blind leap."[197]

Be aware that just because the person making a statement is a well-known scientist does not mean his speculations have validity or are scientific.

Speculation is often preferred to facts when the atheistic worldview is placed under the microscope. Humans can always invent alternative ideas and speculations, for the origin of the universe and life. Even rejection of known science is preferred by some rather than acknowledge a Creator. They hope science will find a more acceptable explanation.[198]

Self-Refuting Statements

Another method used by atheists and other skeptics can be labeled self-refuting statements. That means that though a statement may seem insightful at first glance, it cannot stand logically. This is because if the statement were accepted as true, it would fail the test it declares. The statement fails its own claim.

One author used the cartoon of Wile E. Coyote unintentionally sawing of the tree limb he is sitting on as an illustration of self-refuting statements. This illustrates a self-refuting statement because his action defeats his own intention.[199] So a self-refuting statement defeats its intention. An example of a self-refuting statement would be to say, "I cannot speak a word of English" I undermine or disprove the validity of the statement in saying it. The statement itself contradicts what is being asserted.

Here are a few specific examples of self-refuting statements: 'What passes for truth is merely personal opinion.' (This cannot pass for truth as it is also merely a personal opinion). 'No one knows what is true' (Then how do you know this is true?) 'Reality is merely a construct of the human mind.' (This statement is also a construct of the human mind, so why should we believe it?), 'Truth cannot be communicated;' (This is an attempt to communicate truth).

More examples: 'Everything is an illusion.' (This assumes we have some basis for evaluating and recognizing the difference between illusion and reality. If everything were an illusion, there would be no means of discovering it because the illusions would be all we had.)[200] 'We can never be certain about anything.' (Are you certain about that? This is a claim to be certain about something. If we can be certain or sure about that statement, we are certain about something and the statement is therefore false).[201]

A few more: 'Everything is meaningless.' (If true, those words would have no meaning.) 'No one knows anything about God.' (This is a claim to know something about God! How does someone know God is unknowable?) Also, if someone admits they know nothing about God, they cannot know that you know nothing about God, unless you admit to that.

Some skeptics may attempt to evade the logic of the contradiction in any of such statements by saying they are not claiming it is either true or false. If he says that, his statement is still false because it is a hidden assumption that 'we know that we cannot know.' This is also self-contradictory.[202]

Christian apologist Ravi Zacharias, was at a scientific meeting. He asked the scientists if it was correct that they held that only what could be proven by scientific method or mathematics could be true. They agreed. This would, of course, exclude God by definition and assumptions instead of by evidence, logic or reasoning.

Zacharias then asked how that statement could then be true since it could not be proven by scientific method or by mathematics. He said an embarrassed silence ensued. Finally one scientist admitted that "We sometimes cheat on our philosophy."

It is important to recognize the limits of science. There is no way to prove by the methods of science that only those methods can verify reality. Which of those would you use in an attempt to prove that God does not exist? Neither math nor application of the scientific method would apply. It is impossible to prove that only that which can be verified by science exists or is real.

In "Religion: Reality or Substitute" C.S. Lewis wrote: *"Authority, reason, experience; on these three, mixed in varying proportions all our knowledge depends."*[203] We all, including scientists, rely upon ways of knowing in addition to reason as applied in science and math.

If someone tells you science has proven God's non-existence, ask how science has done that. What methods or research was used? Do not let such false statements

61

intimidate you. Science has no method or tools to prove the non-existence of God.

The Reality of Pain and Evil

Another argument atheists and others make is that a good and all-powerful God cannot exist because of the reality of evil. They proclaim that such a God would not allow war, children to starve to death, or people to be tortured or calamities etc.

This type of argument includes a number of hidden assumptions. It is an emotional and illogical argument because atheists claim there is no God, yet think they know what he would be like if he did exist. They assume He would agree with them and that they would understand His purposes and plans.

Atheists assume to know the difference between good and evil and use an absolute standard of morality to judge God, yet deny any ultimate standard of morality exists. Without an absolute standard by which to justify the criticism they make of God, their statements have no basis, and no validity.[204] As C.S. Lewis admitted after giving up atheism:

"My argument against God was that the universe seemed so cruel and unjust. But how had I got this idea of just and unjust? A man does not call a line crooked unless he has some idea of a straight line. What was I comparing this universe with when I called it unjust?"[205]

Unless absolute moral standards are real, this argument against God merely reflects a personal preference, or opinion. It is important to recognize this contradiction. The critic assumes an absolute moral standard by which to refute the validity of claims of an all-powerful and loving God. But they also deny an absolute moral standard exists!

These critics also assume that God, if he existed, would be responsible for evil and that evil serves no meaningful purpose. From an atheistic perspective, they cannot know whether these things are true. Many more irrational and unverifiable assumptions are hidden behind the assertion there is no God.

Evil is a serious problem for atheists. They have no logical explanation for its existence. Declaring it to be a hangover from evolution doesn't work because they claim man is inherently good. Claiming that humanity is good but society is evil does not work. Society is merely a grouping of humans. If humanity was good, society as a collection of good people would be good as well. The other excuses they present are just as invalid. Atheism has no means of resolving evil without depriving man of his essence.

The actual God who exists gave man free will and responsibility for his and her use of that freedom. To have free will requires that we can choose to do good or choose to do evil. God allows evil to be done but is not cause. There is a huge difference between allowing and causing something. If God prevented evil from occurring we would not have free will. If He prevented the consequences of evil there would be no reason to stop doing evil or mature in moral reasoning and behavior. Most of what we consider to be evil in the world is clearly the responsibility of human choices.

According to the Bible, everything on the planet has been affected by the fall of man. All disease, the violence in the physical world, including natural disasters are consequences of man's rebellion against God. Nature itself has been contaminated and distorted by the consequences of human sin.[206]

Could it be true that nature, which was intended to be under human stewardship, is rebelling against us as we rebelled against its Creator? There are many detailed presentations that reveal more completely the fallacies and hidden assumptions of the atheist's arguments relating to the existence of evil.[207]

The existence of evil and suffering is actual evidence that the Biblical Christian worldview is the truth. Evil or sin is obvious and the Bible contains the only adequate explanation of its origin and its resolution or cure. As former atheist G.K. Chesterton wrote a century ago,

"Modern masters of science are much impressed with the need of beginning all inquiry with a fact. The ancient masters of religion were equally impressed with that necessity. They began with the fact of sin. ..."[208]

Chesterton went on to say that despite human inclinations to deny it, we can see the reality of sin everywhere and it is therefore readily provable.[209] The reality of sin and evil validates the Biblical message, that humans are all sinners. The desire to deny and avoid this truth is one of the actual causes for atheism. Even though widely denied, it is certainly one of the most obvious of biblical truths.

Atheism cannot be proven by logic because the rules of logic state universal negatives cannot be proven. The statement, 'There is no God' is a universal negative and therefore cannot be proven by logic.[210] Logic cannot prove the existence of God either. Reason evaluating argument and evidence, however, demonstrates that belief in God is more rational than unbelief.

Related to this is that the claim to know there is no God is a claim to know too much. No human knows all that can possibly be known. Neither is it correct to say that we definitely have either the ability or methods to absolutely prove His non-existence.

Three men eating at a restaurant next to my wife and I declared themselves to be atheists when I informed them I was a Christian. They began a jovial banter with me attempting to show that belief in God was unreasonable. Finally, as we all left the restaurant together, I said, "No one knows enough to be an honest atheist." That ended our conversation. Whether that was the right thing to say at that moment, I'm not sure, but I am sure it is true.

It is interesting that several places in the Bible declare that if someone genuinely wants to know the true God He will reveal Himself to them.[211]

Scientific Arguments for Atheism

Atheists claim to base their position upon science. However, modern science would never have developed from atheistic assumptions. Atheism requires a universe developing by random accident and chance. Modern science is based upon a universe of design and consistency. Science requires reliably consistent principles that can be discovered and utilized in research and technology. It is not a random universe.

There are some seemingly random elements such as the diffusion of gases. However, that too, proves to be evidence of design. If gasses did not diffuse or disperse into the surrounding air we would exhale once and then be chocked to death by our own re-inhaled carbon dioxide.

Some events may appear to be random, but we are discovering that they too serve a purpose and are elements of design. They prove to be evidence the earth was designed with humans in mind. Atheism contradicts the basis of science as well as many specific discoveries of modern science.

The so-called scientific arguments against the existence of God are very weak. Physicist Hugh Ross mentions that prior to the twentieth century and telescopes that can see beyond the Milky Way, some scientists and philosophers complained that the universe was too small to be the work of an infinite all-powerful God. Now that the universe appears to be nearly infinite they complain that it is too huge to serve merely as humanities home.[212] Obviously, the size of the universe is not the issue.

A related argument is the claim that the vastness of the universe and the relative smallness of the earth proves that we would be insignificant to a God if one exists. Assuming that spiritual significance and value would be determined by size is a misguided assumption.[213] It is much like the nonsense of assuming a 300 pound man is of greater spiritual significance and value than a 150 pound one.

These are philosophical and metaphysical assumptions, not science. The immensity of the universe can just as easily be considered as evidence revealing the awesomeness of God's power and genius to all who will see.[214] The size of the universe may also serve His purposes in ways we do not yet fathom.

Another of these supposedly scientific arguments is that if there is no life elsewhere in the universe it proves we are just an accident that developed on a planet suitable for such to occur. If no life is found to exist elsewhere in the universe, the atheist's argument would be that, *"We were alone in an infinite desert. Which just showed the absurdity of the Christian idea that there was a Creator who was interested in living creatures."*[215]

The asserted argument is of course an unprovable assumption. It would be at least as valid to assume that life only existing here was due to a unique situation and plan by the Creator, who made this planet suitable for life as we know it.

On the other hand, it has been argued by atheists that if we find life in outer space, it will somehow prove that we are not unique and not a special concern of God. It is declared that life elsewhere, *"… just showed (equally well) the absurdity of Christianity with its parochial idea that Man could be important to God."*[216] It would only be parochial if it is not of God

Such arguments reveal a basic dishonesty. No matter what the truth proves to be, they have an argument in advance. Attempting to justify atheism is what matters, not the scientific truth. Actually, neither of these arguments disprove the existence of God nor the validity of Christianity. They are merely assertions and interpretations based upon prior assumptions. The Bible deals specifically with life on our planet. It is silent about what God may have done or be doing elsewhere. God has not chosen to let us know what He has been doing from eternity.[217]

C.S. Lewis wrote that, *"the odd thing is that both these hypotheses are used as grounds for rejecting Christianity ... We treat God as the police treat a man when he is arrested; whatever He does will be used in evidence against Him."*[218]

The opponents of theism are attempting to have all bases covered so that whatever proves to be true will seem to support them. As C.S. Lewis pointed out:

"Each new discovery, even every new theory is held at first to have the most wide-reaching theological and philosophical consequences. It is seized by unbelievers as the basis for a new attack on Christianity. ..."[219]

These new discoveries are extensively promoted along with the arguments how they prove Christianity to be false, or evolution to be true or prove God does not exist. Then, as more serious study and thorough analysis takes place, the attacks and claims are found to be baseless or completely fraudulent. The problem is that some people hear the criticisms and attacks, but they don't hear the corrections so they continue to believe the false statements. Perhaps that is the motive for repeating the same approach again and again with each discovery because some people are convinced of the claims not realizing they have been proven false.

A recent example was the claims of a transitional bird fossil found in China. An extensive article in National Geographic heralded the find. When it was found to be a forgery a small retraction was made in the magazine a few months later.

One argument for the earth being billions of years old in order to allow time for evolution is the thickness of the ice sheets in Greenland and the Antarctic. However, Dr. Jake Herbert notes that *"if current average snowfall rates have always been the norm, then the Greenland ice sheet could form in about 5,000 years and the Antarctic in a little more than 10,000 years, ignoring factors such as melting. Of course, melting would increase the ice sheet formation time, but higher snowfall rates would decrease the time."*[220]

Hebert points out that the dating of the annual amount of snow and ice deposited is based upon assumptions that cannot be proven, but that are interpreted so as to give apparent support to old earth theories.[221]

A newer argument based upon DNA research by evolutionists is that chimpanzee and human DNA is 96 to 98 percent similar. These figures however, result from carefully selecting which data to use in such reports. This is a method of making science seem supportive of one's biases. According to research reported in the <u>American Journal of Human Genetics,</u> only about two-thirds of chimps DNA sequence can be precisely matched to human DNA.[222] More thorough reporting of research diminishes the appearance of similarity.

Some will argue that if God created the world and universe why is there such evidence of flaws, faulty operation and imperfect design? In regard to this criticism from atheist Jay Gould, William Dembski states that since Gould doesn't know the designer's objectives, he cannot actually know if the design is flawed or imperfect.[223]

Furthermore, the Bible informs us that the entire planet was affected and infected with the results of man's rebellion against God. Perfection was destroyed. Sin radically affected all of the physical creation including the human body. Deterioration, death, deformity and disease began.

The environment of the earth was greatly changed due to the fall of man. As the relationship between God and man was altered, so were all other relationships. This includes the relationship between man and the earth for which we were given responsibility. *"The creation was subjected to futility"* and *"bondage to decay"* by the Creator. The original patterns on the planet were disrupted. (See Genesis 3:14-24; 7:6-8:22; Isa. 24:1, 4; Jer. 4:23-28; 12:4; Rom. 8:19-23).

A former evolutionist wrote about informing a class he was teaching about the sightless fish in the darkness of Mammoth Cave. These fish have what appears to be embryonic eyes.

The teacher explained the theory that they have lost the ability to see because of living in the darkness of the cave for eons. When he finished a student asked how he knew these fish ever had the ability to see. The teacher admitted that he did not really know. He came to realize, that despite the theory no one actually knows whether those fish ever had the capacity to see.[224]

The Argument of Vestigial Organs

In the past, science was alleged to prove evolution by the existence of 'vestigial organs.' By vestigial was meant some organ that had been useful during the past evolution of the animal, but that had become useless or nearly useless now in humans. That organ was supposedly no longer necessary, but had not yet disappeared. *"The list of vestigial organs in humans has shrunk from about 180 in 1890 to 0 [in] 1999."*[225]

This could be labeled another type of argument from silence. The purpose or function of certain organs in the body was unknown in the past. Evolutionists assumed there was no longer a function for those organs and that they therefore proved evolution had occurred. Dembski mentions that the phrase 'vestigial' was really a cloak for our earlier lack of knowledge of the function of various organs.[226] As knowledge increased in the fields of anatomy and physiology, the list of vestigial organs soon diminished. Now this argument as a proof of evolution is usually considered invalid,[227] though some scientists and science textbooks continue to present it as if it is true.

For example, in 2007, Francisco Ayala, President of the American Association for the Advancement of Science wrote, *"The human vermiform appendix is a functionless vestige of a fully developed organ present in other animals."* **He added that such organs** *"argue against creation by design but are fully understandable as a result of evolution by natural selection."*[228] **It is astounding that such a ranking scientist could seem to be so ignorant of the knowledge of human anatomy and physiology.**

A challenge to Darwinism's naïve view of the appendix was issued by the Duke University Medical School in 2007. One use of the appendix is as a location for the *"beneficial bacteria living in the human gut."*[229]

Scientific American received an inquiry in 1999 whether the human appendix was vestigial or not. Loren Martin, Professor of physiology at Oklahoma State University was asked by the journal to respond. In answer Martin wrote, *"For years, the appendix was credited with very little physiological function. We now know, however, the appendix serves an important role in the fetus and in young adults. Endocrine cells appear in the appendix of the fetus at around the 11th week of development."*[230]

He goes on to explain that these cells produce important biological compounds. Thus the appendix plays an early role in the human Immune system. Martin added that the lack of evidence for this in animal research was because domestic animals do not have an appendix. More recent research confirms that the appendix also plays a significant role in maintaining the healthy operation of the digestive system.[231]

William Parker, assistant professor of surgical sciences at Duke University suggested it was perhaps time to correct the biology textbooks in the light of recent discoveries. Many science texts still list the appendix as a vestigial organ.[232]

However, this is not the perspective of all scientists. Emeritus professor of Biology at the University of Chicago, Jerry Coyne writing in 2009 declared, *"We humans have many vestigial features proving we evolved. The most famous is the appendix."*[233] At that late date he must have known it was not true. Apparently the dogma of evolution is more important than scientific facts.

As Jerry Bergman explains, *"Evidently to salvage this once-critical support for evolution, a new revisionist definition of vestigial structure is now sometimes used."*[234] Bergman explains that the new definition is vague enough so almost any structure in humans could be labeled vestigial: *"a vestigial organ is any part of an organism that has diminished in size during its evolution because the function it served decreased in importance or became totally unnecessary."*[235]

From this new definition, Isaac Isimov claimed two examples of vestigial organs in humans. Bergman explains that Isimov declared that, *"the tiny bones posterior to the sacrum called the coccyx" as "once meant for a tail" and "the small muscles around the ears (which Isimov claims are 'unworkable muscles once meant to move the ears'). ...these conclusions are not based on empirical evidence but instead on evolutionary assumptions."*[236]

A medical site explains the importance of the coccyx in contrast to Isimov's claims: *"In the human body, the coccyx serves a variety of important functions, including as an attachment site for various muscles, ligaments and tendons."*[237] **The site adds that the coccyx also serves a weight bearing function when we are sitting.**

This new redefinition of vestigial is not consistently applied. For example, our jaw and nostrils are smaller than those in our assumed evolutionary ancestors as is our brow ridges and front limbs (arms).[238] **This indicates the redefinition of 'vestigial' as an effort to save evolution is only applied by evolutionists when it is convenient and ignored otherwise. That is not legitimate science but the selective application of imagination.**

<u>Microevolution Is Not Macroevolution</u>

The only actual evidence for the assumed macroevolution (from the single cell to humans) is microevolution (adaptation to the environment within a particular life group or species). What Darwin actually saw was the variation within a species. He extrapolated (imagined) change from one species to another from those observations and evolutionists have continued this imagination.

Maciej Giertych, Geneticist with the Polish Academy of Sciences wrote, *"Perhaps the most evident misinformation in textbooks is the suggestion that microevolution is a small-scale example of macroevolution."*[239] **Giertych continues,**

"The misinformation lies in concealing the fact that select adopted populations are poorer (fewer alleles) than the unselected natural populations from which they arose ... Microevolution, formation of races is a fact. Populations adapt to specific environments with the more successful alleles increasing in numbers and others declining or disappearing all together. Change can also occur due to accidental loss of alleles (genetic drift) in small populations. Both amount to decline in genetic information. Macroevolution requires its increase."[240]

Giertych is informing us that science proves the assumed mechanism for macroevolution does not and cannot occur! He is saying mutations occur because of the loss of information in the cells, not an increase as macroevolution requires.

Dr. Lee Spetner a biophysicist formerly of Johns Hopkins University agrees with Giertych's conclusion. Spetner analyzed examples of mutations that evolutionists have claimed to have been increases in information in his book <u>Not By Chance</u>. Spetner showed those mutations are actually cases of the loss of specificity. This is a loss of information rather than an increase. He wrote, *"All point mutations that have been studied on the molecular level turn out to reduce the genetic information and not to increase it."*[241]

The famous French zoologist Pierre-Paul Grasse is an evolutionist, but published a devastating expose proving Darwinism does not work. From his vast research, he *"insists that mutations are only trivial changes; they are merely the result of slightly altered genes, whereas 'creative evolution ... demands the genesis of new ones.'"*[242] **Grasse also emphasized that mutations have definite fixed boundaries that cannot ever be crossed and declared that it could not be emphasized enough that variation and evolution are not the same thing.**

Dr. Spetner went on to state that: *"The neo-Darwinists would like us to believe that large evolutionary changes can result from a series of small events if there are enough of them. But if these events all lose information they can't be the steps in the kind of evolution the NDT [Neo-Darwinian theory] is supposed to explain,* *no matter how many mutations there are. Whoever thinks macroevolution can be made by mutations that lose information is like the merchant who lost a little money on each sale but thought he could make it up in volume."*[243]

Giertych has also written that, "*Genetics has no proof for evolution. It has trouble explaining it. The closer one looks at the evidence for evolution, the less one finds of substance. In fact the theory keeps on postulating evidence and failing to find it, moves on to other postulates (fossils, missing links, natural selection of improved forms, positive mutations, molecular phylogenic sequences etc.). This is not science.*"[244]

Most mutations are negative and many are lethal. Mutations can develop a new variation of the original but do not result in the development of a more complex or more advanced form of living things. A recent example was the development of an orange cauliflower, a variation within that type or species of plant. It is still a cauliflower, an example of microevolution, not an advance to a more advanced life form.

Microevolution, change within a species or class of organisms, is the only genuine type of evolution,[245] **But microevolution is not all that evolutionists claim has occurred. Microevolution is variation to adapt to different environments. The organism involved is a variation of the same kind, not a more advanced form of life.**[246] **The process of microevolution indicates that macroevolution cannot occur. There are proven limits beyond which change cannot occur. Just ask any animal breeder. These facts are ignored and hidden by evolutionists. Microbiologist Michael Denton declares that,**

"*...the only aspect of his [Darwin's] theory which has received any support over the past century is where it applies to microevolutionary phenomena. His general theory, that all life on earth had originated and evolved by a gradual successive accumulation of fortuitous mutations, is still, as it was in Darwin's time, a highly speculative hypothesis entirely without direct factual support and very far from the self-evident axiom some of its more aggressive advocates would have us believe.*"[247]

One book review of Spetner's **Not By Chance** is titled, "Evolution: Science or Religion?" The reviewer states that *"Spetner claims research finding like these that don't fit approved doctrine are simply ignored by evolutionary biologists."*[248] The reviewer also stated,

"The book relates how stunning advances in biotechnology in just the past two decades have dramatically widened the gulf separating the realities of empirical science from the myths of neo-Darwinism."[249]

D.W. Mackay quotes Julian Huxley's argument from **The Humanist Frame**, that *"in the evolutionary pattern of thought there is no longer either need or room for the supernatural."*[250]

This 'evolutionary pattern of thought' is not scientifically credible, but is a modern myth held by blind faith. It is based upon misperceptions and major misinterpretations of science that result from flawed worldview assumptions.

Dr. Raymond Damadian, inventor of the MRI, stated that a Scientist looks, *"at the experiments he is performing under conditions he himself is manipulating, and jumps to the conclusion that he thinks he understand how creation took place, and that God wasn't necessary. This becomes the root of atheism, and it got hold of me."* He went on to explain his change in perspective. *"For me now the true thrill of science is the search to understand a small part of God's grand design."*[251]

Damadian's words contradict Dawkins sarcastic statement referred to earlier that acknowledging a Creator eliminates the motivation for scientific investigation. Damadian is one of an increasing number of scientists who have recognized that no field of science actually supports macroevolution. Instead science is increasingly leading us to the awareness of the Grand Designer.

God established order and design throughout His creation. It is evidence of His existence when scientists discover some of the consistently reliable principles that He has established in creating and sustaining the universe.[252] How could the evident consistency of such principles and design of the universe be the result of randomness and chance? Attempts to correlate these contradictory concepts as if they fit together are irrational.

Atheism is Held By Faith

Since atheism cannot be proven, it is assumed, believed on the basis of faith despite increasing evidence to the contrary. This is not something atheists want to admit. Dawkins and other atheists specifically deny that their convictions are based upon faith, but they are not being candid. Atheists ignore their basic presuppositions that are flawed, and ignore scientific knowledge that is inconvenient. The alleged scientific basis for their unbelief is non-existent. They must focus their efforts on attempts to disprove, evade and deny the arguments and evidences for God's existence.

This was confirmed by South African Physicist Louw Alberts as stated in a 1989 interview, *"There is nothing scientific about the viewpoint of an atheist. To say it all happened by chance cannot be proved or disproved. It is a statement of faith."*[253] Atheists claim that a theory or explanation that is impossible to falsify (disprove) or verify cannot be true when they are referring to creation. They then promote atheism as true though it fails their own test because it cannot be verified or falsified. This, however, may change as science is giving increasing evidence that supports creation and diminishes the possible validity of atheism.

Evaluating Arguments

One argument we considered earlier against belief in God is that psychological and sociological theories can explain all beliefs A flaw in these arguments is, however, that they themselves can be explained by psychological and sociological theories. If the theories are valid despite the fact they can be explained psychologically and sociologically, then belief in God is still valid despite being able to be explained that way. So the argument may prove why some people believe as they do, it does nothing to prove there is no God. [254]

The atheist Geoffry Berg acknowledges in his book, <u>The Six Ways Of Atheism</u> that psychological and sociological theories cannot prove there is no God. He wrote that the psychological arguments used to explain humanity's belief in God, even if true, do not prove that God may not still exist.[255] Berg's point is of huge significance. The popular argument by Feuerbach that God is merely a psychological invention of the human mind is an unverifiable assertion that would not disprove God's existence even it were verifiable.

Similar arguments by Freud and Marx, explain where some ideas about God arose but do not disprove His existence.[256] God can still exist outside these conceptions of the mind. Using their reasoning, one can also dismiss Feuerbach's, Marx's and Freud's arguments as merely inventions of the human mind and therefore invalid. This argument defeats itself.

Marx makes the mistake of assuming that because religion has been used to control and exploit humans, that was the reason for its origin. Humans have proven themselves adept at twisting the best things into evil purposes. Religion has been used for both good and evil purposes. Neither use proves or disproves the existence of God.

In addition, Marx's argument that religion was conceived in order to control the masses can be answered by showing it has also been used to oppose oppression. Examples are the abolition of slavery in the British Empire, the abolition of suttee (wife burning) in India,[257] and the abolition of cannibalism in Irian Java and many other places.[258]

Commenting about the efforts to discredit especially Christianity, Dr. Alberts declared, *"Those people haven't the courage to admit the tremendous advances that Christianity gave us. … People tend to ignore the incredible, immeasurable contributions of Christianity to mankind and will only look at the negative evidence of what the Christian Church has been responsible for."*[259]

Similarly, Freud argues in <u>The Future of an Illusion</u> that religion is the expression of longing for a Father figure that only continues because it meets some psychological need. Though his argument may often be valid, it does not disprove God's existence. If God exists, would not faith in Him and worship of Him meet some psychological need as well as other needs?[260] St Augustine wrote, *"You have made us for yourself O God, and our hearts are restless until they find their rest in you."* Augustine recognized the need for God to be psychological as well as spiritual.

Lepp declares *"I have too severely criticized the Freudian pretension of seeing in religious faith only a neurotic pattern of behavior to fall into the temptation of applying a similar reductive method to unbelief."* [261]

He is saying we cannot dismiss either belief or unbelief in God as nothing more than psychological phenomenon. We cannot prove nor disprove the existence of a Supreme Being by these arguments.

Efforts to refute arguments for the existence of God reveal another weakness in atheism. Were atheists to succeed in refuting specific arguments for God's existence, it would merely refute those arguments. It would not prove God to be non-existent nor prove atheism to be true. It is like having refuted the testimony of a witness to a crime. The refuted testimony does not prove the crime did not occur. It merely refutes that particular witness's testimony.

Atheists who are consistent, acknowledge that without God, life has no genuine or ultimate meaning or purpose. Frederick Nietzsche and John-Paul Sartre declared in their writings that there was no God and therefore there could be no real meaning or purpose to life. They went on to say that since humans could not live without a sense of purpose that it was necessary to make up some cause, reason or purpose for living.[262]

"The French philosopher Jean-Paul Sartre taught that man had been dumped into a meaningless universe and was caught

between the absurdity of life's origin and the fear of life's extinction."[263]

If there were no God and no ultimate meaning to existence, why could humanity not accept that reality? The need for a sense of meaning and purpose is a clue. Instead of accepting the atheistic point of view, it seems more rational and logical to assume that our need for meaning is because we were created to have meaning and purpose.

The fact that atheism cannot be proven but is held by faith; the atrocities governments carry out when they assume there is no God; and the reality that humans struggle to survive without some sense of ultimate meaning and purpose are clues that there must be a God. But there are also strong arguments for a Creator and against atheism from science.

Though it is often claimed that science has destroyed any basis for believing in God and Christianity, and that science supports atheism, these assertions can be readily proven to be false. Atheist Geoffry Berg admits:

"... the arguments concerning scientific disproof of God and the human psychology arguments are not valid arguments against the existence of God. ... The problem with such arguments is that while they rightly discredited religions and disproved the truth of religious scriptures, they did not disprove the existence of a monotheistic God as such."[264]

Berg assumes that scientific arguments have eliminated any reason for accepting the validity of all religions and religious scriptures, but he is wrong. My earlier book, <u>The Uniqueness of the Christian Faith</u> gives evidence that the biblical writings and the biblical faith are radically different from the world religions.

There are also many books presenting solid evidence that we have an authentic text of the Bible and that the Bible is historically reliable. A few of these books are listed at this endnote.[265] Those books demonstrate there is extensive evidence and rational reasons for embracing the Christian Faith.

Intolerance of Atheists

Growing evidence from science actually supports the belief that there must be a God. There are numerous scientific discoveries that invalidate both atheism and its basis, evolution. The actual problem, Dr. Dennis Swift, a former evolutionist states, is that *"Scientists often ignore or discard information that does not fit their preconceived ideas of man's development."*[266]

When ignoring information is deemed an insufficient response, the scientific establishment will attack the credibility, credentials, reputation, or motives of the one they view as an enemy. They have made up false excuses for getting the person removed from any position of influence in[267] the secular realm.

A flagrant example of removing scientists who disagree with the theory of evolution is that of former Iowa State University Astrophysicist Guillermo Gonzalez. He was denied tenure for writing a book on Intelligent Design, <u>The Privileged Planet</u>. One of those voting against tenure admitted that was the cause. But the official reasons were his lack of peer reviewed publications, lack of citations in other scientific papers and lack of grant money he received.

In reality Gonzalez lead all ISU astronomers in citations in scientific papers since 2001 and published over 350% more that the number of peer reviewed publications required for tenure. He also received more than three times the amount of grant money attributed to him from NASA alone, not to mention other grants. Though trying to evade the evidence, ISU was clearly discriminating against Dr. Gonzalez for his advocacy of Intelligent Design.[268]

Another specific example of this was presented in the TV documentary titled "The Mysterious Origin of Man" which aired on NBC twice in 1996. Dr. Virginia Steen McIntyre, PHD in Geology was with the U.S. Geological Society doing field work in Mexico.

Her specialty is volcanic ash research used to help date archaeological sites. Her conclusions about the dates of discovered spear points being much earlier than the accepted dates were backed up by two other USGS team members. But her findings were considered controversial and did not agree with mainstream science. Her unwillingness to alter the data to agree with the previously accepted dates resulted in her being dismissed from the Geological Society. Her contract to teach at a state university was also cancelled

The Documentary mentioned that much scientific information is never revealed to the public because it fails to confirm accepted theories. It also told that McIntyre was prevented from gaining another position in her scientific field.[269] Scientific Journals came up with excuses not to publish the scientific data that backed up her claims. She later wrote, *"So there I was in 1981, stonewalled, jobless, no career, damaged reputation ... For thirteen years I dropped out of science completely."*[270]

More recent research at the site by others in 2004 and 2006 appears to validate her original dating.[271] Mainstream scientists have refused to accept the validity of the information because it contradicts their views. The alleged objectivity and pursuit of truth in science is not always a reality. Bias and discrimination are frequently experienced by scientist who do not adhere to the official propaganda.

An older example of this bias against scientific data that did not fit the prescribed views of the scientific elite is the case of Immanuel Velikovsky. His unorthodox scientific theories and evidence supporting them entitled, Worlds in Collision created huge controversy even prior to publication. Harpers Magazine and Readers Digest had given favorable presentations on it in advance.

When Macmillan published the book in 1950, a prominent scientist threatened to organize a boycott of Macmillan's science textbooks, so the book was quickly transferred to Doubleday which did not publish science textbooks.[272] Once published it quickly became a best seller. Despite being difficult to imagine, the book was banned at a number of academic institutions here in the U.S.[273]

<u>Worlds in Collision</u> met with such opposition and hostility in scientific circles because it presented theories and evidence that contradicted two sacred cows of the scientific establishment. It called into question the validity of uniformitarian geology and Darwinian evolution.[274] The book eventually resulted in establishing what is now known as modern scientific catastrophism.[275]

Six years later Velikovsky published <u>Earth In Upheaval</u> presenting conclusive geological verification of his theories.[276] In that book's preface he explained: "*I have excluded from [this writing] all references to ancient literature, traditions and folklore; and this I have done with intent, so that careless critics cannot decry the entire work as 'tales and legends.' Stones and bones are the only witness.*"[277]

The website, <knowledge.co.uk> indicates criticism of Velikovsky's works, (much inaccurate), has given the erroneous idea that Velikovsky has been proven completely in error.[278] Mainstream science has now adopted some of Velikovsky's conclusions.

A few more examples of the intolerant attitude toward criticism of evolution follow.[279] February 2003, Chemistry professor and head of the Division of Science and Mathematics at Mississippi University for Women, Nancy Bryson was released from her position after a lecture on scientific criticisms of Darwinism for a group of honors students.[280]

In 2005 Dr. Caroline Crocker, a cell biologist, was reprimanded, and pulled from her lecture duties at George Mason University. Her contract was not renewed because she presented several slides about Intelligent Design as an alternative theory. Crocker said: "*Students are not allowed to question Darwinism. There are universities where they poll students on what they believe and single them out.*"[281] **Obviously,** professors are not allowed to question Darwin either. This type of intellectual straitjacket violates the purpose of a university and stifles critical thinking.

August 2004, an article espousing Intelligent Design by Stephen Meyer was published in the peer reviewed **Proceedings of the Biological Society of Washington**, which is affiliated with the Smithsonian. The journal's editor, evolutionary biologist Richard Sternberg had his scientific career threatened by his Smithsonian supervisors for publishing the article.[282] See Sternberg's own statement regarding this situation.[283]

Claudia Wallace wrote in a **Time** magazine article "The Evolution Wars," that allowing the mention of Intelligent Design or scientific criticism of evolution, *"strikes horror into the hearts of scientists and science teachers across the U.S. not to mention plenty of civil libertarians."*[284]

The major reason for this horror is the pretense and proclamation by evolutionists that Intelligent Design is merely religion and not science. When genuine scientists and professors present evidence contradicting evolution, fear arises that adults and students may realize that intelligent design is based on real science, not religion and that it is macroevolution that is not scientifically validated nor defensible.

Another reason for the horror among atheistic scientists is that more and more scientists are speaking out about their skepticism regarding the evidence and credibility of the evolutionary theory.

Biologist, Richard Dawkins pretends there is no scientific element to the debate, *"I'm concerned about implying that there is some sort of scientific argument going on. There's not."*[285] **There most certainly is a scientific debate going on** *"because the materialist story is false and, further, is contradicted by mounting physical evidence in physics, chemistry and biology."*[286]

In addition, the book by Australian microbiologist Michael Denton, **Evolution: A theory In Crisis** demolishes the scientific credibility of macroevolution and Dawkins pretenses. Dawkins also dishonestly tries to paint Einstein as an atheist,[287] despite Einstein's statements clearly demonstrating belief in a Creator.[288] In an interview Einstein declared *"I'm not an atheist."*[289] Other statements Einstein made would seem to justify calling him a Deist.[290]

Dawkins is in complete denial of the facts. There are scientists all over the world questioning the validity of evolution. Denton has stated that skepticism regarding the validity of macroevolution, *"has been generally more marked on the European continent than in the English speaking world."*[291]

Intelligent design is based upon an increasing amount of scientific evidence. If there was genuine objectivity in science as to origins, Intelligent Design would be considered and taught along with any other theoretical model.

Henry Schaefer, is a Chemist at the University of Georgia, and Nobel Prize nominee five times. He has encouraged the need for debate on evolution. He is among one hundred U.S. scientists who signed a "Scientific Dissent on Darwinism." *"'Some defenders of Darwinism,' says Schaefer, 'embrace standards of evidence for evolution that as scientists they would never accept in other circumstances."*[292] Once again the lack of scientific objectivity in defending evolution is exposed.

Richard Dawkins reveals another tactic of atheists deceptively criticizing advocates of Intelligent Design for not playing, *"by the rules of science. They do not publish papers in peer reviewed journals and their hypothesis cannot be tested by research and the study of evidence."*[293]

Dawkins criticism is invalid as he well knows. The scientific journals are headed by evolutionists who routinely refuse to publish scientific papers espousing alternatives to evolution. A rare exception to this exclusion from scientific journals was the earlier referred to article by Stephen Meyer which had severe repercussions for the editor who allowed it to be published. [294] Not only is that true, but the other part of Dawkins statement is deceptive as well. Neither atheism nor evolution can be validated by research and both are contradicted by evidence. He is completely misleading his students and readers.

As Michael Denton observes, *"Darwin's model of evolution is still very much a theory and still very much in doubt when it comes to macroevolutionry phenomena. Furthermore being basically a theory of historical reconstruction, it is impossible to verify by experiment or direct observation as is normal in science."*[295]

Denton further explains: *"Moreover, the theory of evolution deals with a series of unique events, the origin of life, the origin of intelligence and so on. Unique events are unrepeatable and cannot be subjected to any sort of experimental investigation. Such events ... may be the subject of much fascinating and controversial speculation, but their causation can, strictly speaking, never be subject to scientific validation."*[296]

Denton's assessment is correct, however, it is possible to analyze the scientific information available and the arguments of scientists for both evolution and creation to determine which theory is more consistent with the evidence.

The Origin of Intelligent Design

Analyzing the evidence is exactly what Philip Johnson, former law professor at U.C. Berkley did. He had previously accepted the validity of evolution. During a year sabbatical in London he was searching for a research topic. He tells of seeing atheist Dawkin's, book, <u>The Blind Watchmaker</u>, and that of agnostic Microbiologist, Michael Denton's, <u>Evolution: A Theory In Crisis</u> in a bookstore window.

Johnson decided to evaluate the evidence in both books.[297] **His specialization is** *"analyzing the logic of arguments and identifying the assumptions that lie behind those arguments."*[298] **That is exactly the type of specialization needed to effectively evaluate both sides of the issue of origins. Thomas Woodward, writing about Johnson's analysis of the two books mentions Dawkins biased informal logic and that,**

"The key observation that struck Johnson was the way Dawkins, throughout the book, deftly dodged such difficult areas as the fossil record and the Cambrian explosion ..."[299] **He added that Johnson,** *"was amazed at the strength of Denton's case, and he recognized that <u>Evolution: A Theory in Crisis</u> was either 'very, very wrong, or very, very important.'"*[300]

After analyzing the evidence referenced in both books, Johnson pursued more detailed research. His study of the issues involved resulted in losing all confidence in the validity of evolution and become an active advocate of what became known as intelligent design or ID. Phillip Johnson's best known book exposing flaws he discovered in evolution is titled <u>Darwin On Trial</u>. Some other scientists have become convinced through Denton and Johnson to re-evaluate their confidence in evolution and have embraced Intelligent Design. Intelligent Design especially makes sense in the light of recent and current scientific research. Macroevolution fails to correspond to this research and increasing scientific scrutiny.

Evolutionists dismiss the arguments of non-scientists like Johnson, regardless of the validity of the evidence they present. They also attempt to discredit the credentials or reputations of scientists who doubt or reject Darwin. This is because they cannot convincingly refute the scientific evidence these persons are presenting. They will deny that such persons are real scientists or attempt to avoid the evidence by asserting that the arguments are unimportant or that they are religious not scientific.

By such tactics, they are deceiving the public. Despite the evidence against them, some overzealous and misguided scientists declare evolution is a proven scientific fact. They will protect their pet theories against challenges with any means possible.

As we have seen in previous examples, there are advocates of atheism and evolution who will do whatever is necessary to prevent the populace from realizing the emperor has no clothes; that atheism and macro-evolution have no genuine scientific basis.

Thomas Kuhn, author of **The Structure of Scientific Revolutions** approvingly cites **Max Plank who wrote,** "*A new scientific truth does not triumph by convincing its opponents and making them see the light, but rather because its opponents eventually die, and a new generation grows up that is familiar with it.*"[301]

Plank has informed us that scientists are more likely to hold on to their prior beliefs rather than allowing new evidence to revise their thinking.[302] **So much for the pretense of scientific objectivity.**

Part II

Specific examples from science that contradict Atheism.

Cosmology

Some scientists have stated that the ultimate question is, *"Why is there something instead of nothing?"* If you truly start with nothing, where does something come from? Something cannot arise out of nothing by itself. The universe cannot have created itself out of nothing. Without a powerful Creator there would still be nothing!

The Deist, Thomas Paine stated in <u>The Age of Reason</u> (1794) that, "*....everything we behold carries in itself the internal evidence that it did not make itself.*"[303] He is correct. Yet atheists have to assume this happened, which is blind faith not science. There must be someone outside of the universe and prior to it sufficient to account for the origin of the universe.

Alleging that the universe created itself through the laws of physics is like claiming a book review critiquing the plot of a novel created the novel without an author.

The recent movie, "God Is Not Dead" (2014) mentions that to counteract the necessity of a Creator, Stephen Hawking has stated that the universe could create itself because of the law of gravity. Physicist Lawrence Krause assumes in <u>A Universe From Nothing</u>, that the laws of physics could create the universe.[304] These are huge assumptions that do not solve the atheist's problem of origins.

These laws are our mathematical descriptions of how we understand the universe operates. They do not explain how the universe could create itself because there was no means for the operation of these laws until there was a universe of matter and energy. In addition, gravity and these other descriptions of how matter and energy operate had a beginning and source. What is that source? They certainly did not create themselves, but were created to operate along with matter and energy.

Information scientist and engineer Werner Gitt mentions that the laws of nature were not pre-existent but were part of the original creation. That is, they came into being and operation at the time of the origin of the universe.[305]

It is inconceivable that the laws of physics would precede the existence of the physical universe, unless brought into existence by an awesome intelligence to operate as soon as the universe was created. Nothing cannot create anything including the laws of physics. How were these laws established? How is it that these "laws" reflect order and consistency in a supposedly random universe?

Prominent physicist and cosmologist Paul Davies mentioned that the laws of physics are so consistent and predictable they can be defined mathematically. He wrote, *"Few scientists stop to wonder why the fundamental laws of the universe are mathematical."* He noted, *"Most just take it for granted."*[306] Davies could not escape the question *"What is the source of these rational mathematical laws?"* He decided that the only reasonable conclusion was that, *"nature's laws imply a law giving Creator."*[307]

These questions are obstacles to the theory of atheism. The philosophical pronouncements made by atheists are based upon hidden assumptions which remain unacknowledged. Following are some examples of these hidden assumptions.

Time has no creative power it is merely a measurement, so no amount of time by itself will bring something out of nothing. Nor can it create evolution. Without some force or intelligence preceding the universe there would still be nothing. Natural selection requires that there already be something here.

Some scientists are acknowledging that natural selection in the sense of bringing about new or higher life forms has not and does not happen. Natural selection only causes variation within a species that is already in existence. They remain members of the same species as their most ancient ancestors. That variation within a species is what Darwin and others actually have seen. Despite some variations, particularly in the size and shape of their bills, the different finches on the Galapagos Islands remained finches. They did not and cannot develop or morph into something else.[308] As long as finches survive they will always remain finches.

On January 3, 2018 Public TV aired a Nova special on the Hubble telescope. The program explained that Einstein and most scientists back in the early twentieth century had assumed the universe was eternal and limited to our galaxy, the Milky Way. Edwin Hubble however, discovered there were a great many galaxies, each moving away from the others at great speed. This suggested a origin or beginning to the universe.

Earlier Einstein's theory of general relativity indicated to his surprise and dismay that the universe was not eternal but had a beginning. He even added another calculation to his theory he called 'the cosmological constant' in order to support the 'steady state' or eternal, unchanging status of the universe. This made it appear that there was no beginning.

However, another scientist, astronomer Vesto Slipher had shown that other galaxies were moving away from ours. He provided the empirical proof the universe was expanding. Edwin Hubble pointed out Einstein's error and, building upon Slipher's work, verified that the universe is continuing to expand. These discoveries showed the universe had to have had a beginning.

In 1929 Einstein admitted that the additional calculation was the worst mistake of his entire career.[309] He had allowed his prior beliefs to determine his scientific conclusions, which led him to add to the information. The purpose of science is to follow the evidence wherever it leads.

Hubble's discovery that the universe is expanding in all directions from a central point confirmed Einstein's theory verifying that the universe had a point of origin and a beginning. Since the universe had a beginning that meant that something existed outside of and prior to the universe that caused or created the universe. Einstein came to believe in a non-personal Creator because of science.[310]

One of the world's leading astronomers, Alan Sandage spoke at a conference of cosmologists gathered to consider the theological implications of their field. Sandage said, *"that contemplating the majesty of the big bang helped make him a believer in God, willing to accept the that creation could only be explained as a 'miracle.'"*[311]

The evidence from the universe itself makes it seem like the cause or Creator of the universe is extremely powerful, transcendent (existing prior to and outside of what has been created), immaterial and timeless. These characteristics fit well with the biblical portrayal of God. Arno Penzias, Nobel Prize winner in physics stated *"The best data we have (concerning the Big Bang) are exactly what I would have predicted had I nothing to go on but the five books of Moses, the Psalms, the Bible as a whole."*[312]

As many former atheists acknowledge, since there was a beginning, there has to be a powerful creative intelligence to have created the elements and the universe. Without such a powerful creative intelligence there would still be nothing.

Robert Jastrow, scientist and former Director of the Goddard Institute for Space Studies of NASA wrote: *"The details differ, but the essential elements in the astronomical and biblical accounts in Genesis are the same. ...This is an exceedingly strange development, unexpected by all but the theologians. They have always believed the word of the Bible. But we scientists did not expect to find evidence for an abrupt beginning ..."*[313]

Geology: Pleochroic Halos[314]

Pleochroic halos are microscopic effects of radiation in many rocks of the earth's crust. Physicist, Dr. Robert Gentry has extensively studied these halos from a variety of types of radiation. Writing about his research regarding polonium radiation, it was stated that He *"made some amazing discoveries which give evidence of sudden and abrupt origin for the earth."*[315]

He also concluded that the polonium and rocks that had contained it were created simultaneously, and the rocks cooled almost instantaneously. Otherwise there would have been no 'halos' or evidence of the existence of the radiation. Apart from these two conditions being true (simultaneous creation and nearly instantaneous cooling) there would have been no evidence of the prior existence of radioactive polonium in those rocks.[316]

This contradicts the current theories of the earth slowly cooling over millions of years.[317] Gentry used the example of a camera with a flash attachment to take a picture in a completely darkened room. If the flash were to go off before or after the shutter operates, there would be no picture.[318]

The creation of the rocks and radioactivity had to be simultaneous and the cooling very rapid for the picture (the halos) to be there. This caused him to ponder whether it might really be possible after all that the earth was created instantly by Divine fiat or declaration![319] The rate of the decay of polonium and other radioactive substances proves the earth had a beginning and has not been around for billions of years or there would be little or no radioactive material left in existence.[320]

The Anthropic Principle

The Anthropic principle was introduced by astrophysicist and cosmologist Brandon Carter of Cambridge University. This concept refutes the idea of a random universe. A random universe was the foundation of all modern atheistic philosophies. He pointed out that *"life had to be, in effect, 'pre-planned' from the very origin of the cosmos in order to get life to appear..."*[321]

Everything had to be just right from the beginning, including fundamental forces like electromagnetism and gravity to the relative masses of subatomic particles. The slightest variation of a single one of scores of basic values and relationships in nature would have resulted in a very different universe unsuitable for life.[322] In **The Fingerprint of God** astronomer Hugh Ross, formerly an atheist, lists a few of these 'just right' scientific realities that enable life. One of the many examples Ross relates is cited in the endnote.[323]

In **A Brief History of Time**, Steven Hawking, the famous Cambridge theoretical physicist agreed: *"'Why is the universe the way we see it?' The answer is then simple: if it had been different, we would not be here!"*[324] **He continues, referring to the many precise factors science has discovered,** *"The remarkable fact is that the values of these numbers seem to have been very finely adjusted to make possible the development of life. ...it seems clear that there are relatively few ranges of values for the numbers that would allow the development of any form of intelligent life."*[325]

Hawking concludes, *"This means that the initial state of the universe must have been very carefully chosen indeed. ... It would be very difficult to explain why the universe should have begun in just this way, except as an act of a God who intended to create beings like us."*[326]

Former atheist Patrick Glynn agrees, *"Far from being accidental, life appeared to be the goal toward which the entire universe from the very first moment of its existence had been orchestrated, fine tuned."*[327] **Glynn also stated:** *"Secular minded scientists have not been happy with this discovery ... Indeed today the case for design looks very strong."*[328]

The absence of any of a thousand details both vast and minute and there would be no intelligent life on earth; we would not exist. NASA astrophysicist John A. O'Keefe agrees with this assessment. *"If the universe had not been made with the most exacting precision, we could never have come into existence."* **He also said,** *"It is my view that these circumstances indicate the universe was created for man to live in."*[329]

Russian Physicist and mathematician Vladislav Olkhovsky, another former atheist concurs, *"Scientific study of nature gave us formidable stockpiles of data pointing to the fact that fundamental physical constants and general and local properties of the universe are incredibly precise being designed for the sake* of human life."[330] **Olkhovsky added,** "*If the physical constants were slightly different then life would not be possible.*"[331] **These scientists are showing us that reality proves intentional, purposeful design.**

John Polkinghorne, prominent for over thirty years in high energy physics argues against the possibility that amino acids, "*randomly strung themselves together to form the protein chain and strongly asserts that a tightly-knit and intelligible universe such as ours is not sufficiently explained by a random chance process.*"[332]

More recently the field of microbiology has added immensely to the evidence of design. This has become so obvious that many atheists admit the "appearance of design."

"*But by far the most challenging aspect of this new biochemical picture as far as evolution is concerned is the incredible orderliness of all the divisions.*"[333] **There is tremendous order and design throughout nature; not the evidence of increasing complexity and transitional forms we would see were evolution actually true. Despite claims by Dawkins and others: Denton says,** "*No evolutionary biologist has ever produced any quantitative proof that the designs of nature are in fact within the reach of chance.*"[334]

No Science in a Random Universe

The absurdity of atheism and evolution is evident from the very work of scientists who are atheistic. When they devise experiments, develop new technology or send spacecraft to the moon or Mars, they rely upon the order, structure and predictability of nature. Then, when advocating their philosophical beliefs regarding the origin of these principles, they ascribe them to irrational and random chance.

Dembski declares, "*For nature to be an object of inquiry for the scientist, nature must have an order which the scientist can grasp. If nature were totally without form and order, no science would be possible.*"[335]

The inconsistency between an atheist's science and his philosophy is glaring. Modern science arose because of the confidence of early scientists that the universe was orderly, consistent and predictable because it was created by a rational Creator. This confidence enabled scientists to discover how the universe operated and then use that knowledge to do experiments and develop technology. Modern science would never have arisen in the context of belief in a random universe; there would have been no 'natural laws' to discover and no predictability to work with.

Entropy Contradicts Evolution

The law of entropy, also known as the 2nd law of thermodynamics, states that left to itself any physical system will deteriorate or decay. Entropy (disorder) is increasing and the universe is slowly winding down. We see evidence all around us of order and intricate design, yet we also see this order and design is continually deteriorating. Everything in the universe shows the signs of deterioration and degeneration.

This law of physics contradicts the theory and assumed processes of evolution. There is no evidence of increasing design or complexity, in nature as required by the theory.

To justify evolution scientists must conclude that the universe resets itself so as to repeal the effects of this law. There is, however, no evidence of the universe doing so. Where would the incredible power necessary to reset the universe come from? How could a random, mindless universe have such an obvious example of purpose? Resetting to overrule entropy has to be assumed by faith in order to uphold the theory of macroevolution. Science, however, indicates this cannot happen. It would require a vast new input of energy into the universe.

Former atheist and physicist Hugh Ross informs us that the universe is and will continue to expand at an increasingly accelerating rate *"which puts an end to the oscillating universe model ... and means the universe can never contract, therefore it* cannot rebound. This fact eliminates the possibility of a renewal, rebirth or second beginning for the universe."[336]

Ross is saying the expansion of the universe at accelerating speed is itself evidence the universe cannot "reset itself" to counteract the process of entropy.

Another attempt to circumvent the science is to claim that biology is an exception to entropy. However other scientists have pointed out that: *"this does not explain nor answer the question of how it was that such highly organized systems as living organisms could ever come into existence in a world in which irreversible processes always tend to lead to an increase in entropy and thus to disorder."*[337]

We are thus informed that the process of entropy would have prevented the origin of any living organisms by purely natural processes.

Boris Dotsenko, a past Director of Nuclear Physics, Institute of Physics, Kiev, Ukraine, described himself as, *"a convinced atheist, having absorbed Marxist thinking into the very marrow of my bones."*[338] In regard to entropy, Dotsenko said, *"as I thought it through, it occurred to me that as the universe was still intact, there must be an amazingly powerful organizing force at work, keeping the universe controlled and in order. What is more, this force must be non-material or it would disintegrate. Eventually I came to the conclusion that this omnipotent and controlling force was the God of whom the Bible speaks."*[339]

Spontaneous Generation Disproved

The atheist must assume that life somehow spontaneously arose from nonliving matter by random natural processes. Atheist Karl Marx stated that, *"spontaneous generation is the only practical refutation of the theory of creation."*[340]

Louis Pasteur, however, scientifically disproved the theory of spontaneous generation less than two decades after Marx wrote. Pasteur, publishing his work in 1864, established the biogenetic law that life can only arise from life; that nonliving matter cannot produce living matter.[341]

In **Rats, Lice and History**, Hans Zinsaer wrote that, "*The final demonstration by Pasteur, that alleged observations of spontaneous generation were attributable to experimental error marked the ending of biological medievalism.*"[342]

Despite this scientific fact, Biology textbooks portray life as coming from non-living matter. They present the first stage in the development toward life as the accumulation of all the basic necessary compounds in the earth's early oceans.

This merely chemical process is referred to as the "prebiotic soup." It is assumed these compounds over millions of years began to form themselves into proteins and nucleic acids which eventually acquired the ability to self-reproduce. This is presented as if it is scientifically verified to have occurred which it is not.[343] There is actually no means of verifying that it actually occurred. It is another assumption that is necessary for the theory of evolution to be true.

But as **Denton reveals:** "*Considering the way the prebiotic soup is referred to in so many discussions of the origin of life as an already established reality, it comes as something of a shock to realize that there is absolutely no positive evidence for its existence.*"[344]

In other words it is a completely fabricated explanation with no scientific basis except the assumption that evolution must somehow have occurred. This story is imagined as a possible explanation and then presented to the world as if it were a fact.

Dr. George Wald winner of the Nobel Prize, and member of the American Academy of Sciences taught Biology at Harvard for 43 years. He wrote that not only did Pasteur disprove spontaneous generation[345] but also that, "*One has only to contemplate the magnitude of this task to concede that the spontaneous generation of a living organism is impossible.*"[346]

Atheists and evolutionists have to ignore this fundamental law of biology that life only comes from life. As stated before, they come up with a scientific sounding theory and then pretend that it is fact. That enables them to proclaim nonliving matter can somehow produce life. These unprovable assumptions are necessary in order to advocate their belief that no God is required to account for the origin of life. Quoting Olkhovsky again,

"The issue is not only that the spontaneous generation of a single cell cannot find any scientific explanation in the realm of modern physics: the probability of atoms spontaneously molding a protein structure containing just 500 amino acids is $1/10^{950}$ (which is extremely small) while a cell consists of at least 250 different proteins."[347]

He continued, "*No naturalistic working model of life has ever been replicated, not even a minimal self-reproducing cell. So, atheistic statements about naturalistic origin of life with its genetic code and irreducibly complex structure require a more blind faith than the Intelligent Design hypothesis.*"[348]

Olkhovsky presents three conclusions: *"(1) there is no proven scientific fact supporting either progressive macroevolution nor spontaneous generation of biological life. (2) the doctrine of progressive biological macroevolution obviously violates the law of increasing entropy and the second law of thermodynamics. (3) every macroevolutionary doctrine faces an insurmountable gap between humans and apes."*[349]

Einstein agreed no theory of evolution can overcome the gap between animal life and human life. Here again, the basis of atheism is faith. They must assume what science indicates cannot occur somehow did occur.

Bio-Physicist Igor Savich, was raised and educated in Kyrgyzstan as an atheist. He stated in a lecture that regardless of the mutations that occur, and despite tremendous efforts to manipulate the genetics of various life forms, a species remains the same.[350] He is saying the proclaimed mechanism of evolution does not work. All you get is variation within a family or species which is what Darwin actually saw and recorded.

Distinguished University of Massachusetts biologist Lynn Margulis asked the molecular biologists at one of her talks, *"to name a single, unambiguous example of the formation of a new species by the accumulation of mutations. Her challenge goes unmet."*[351] **She also has said that ultimately history will consider neo-Darwinism to be,** *"a minor twentieth century religious sect within the sprawling religious persuasion of Anglo-Saxon biology."*[352]

Design and Irreducible Complexity

In his <u>Origin of the Species</u>, Darwin wrote: *"If it could be demonstrated that any complex organism existed which could not possibly have been formed by numerous, successive, slight modifications, my theory would absolutely break down."* [353]

Biochemist and former evolutionist Michael Behe has demonstrated exactly what concerned Darwin. Behe's research has shown that many of life's building blocks, and organisms are irreducibly complex; that is they 'could not possibly have been formed by numerous successive slight modifications.'

Modern biochemistry was completely unknown until the second half of the twentieth century; one hundred years more recently then Darwin's writings.[354] **Behe writes:** *"Yet for the Darwinian theory of evolution to be true, it has to account for the molecular structure of life. It is the purpose of this book to show that it does not."*[355]

As Behe reveals, molecular chemistry indicates that the building blocks of the individual cell and living systems had to come into existence complete and functional at once or they would not exist[356]**. This points to a Creative Intelligence or God who created the systems complete and functional, enabling the organism to survive and reproduce.**

Michael Behe's book, <u>Darwin's Black Box</u> (1996) created a firestorm among scientists. It argues that complex structures such as proteins cannot be assembled over time bit by bit but like a mousetrap, all the elements must be present simultaneously and working together or the protein does not exist. Each element of the protein requires the presence of all the other elements at the same time for its formation.

Behe goes on to ask, *"What has caused complex systems to form? No one has ever explained in detailed, scientific fashion how mutation and natural selection could build the complex, intricate structures discussed in this book."*[357]

This is true as well for entire bodily systems. Examples include the circulatory system, the system for absorbing nutrients from the environment, and the reproductive system without which that species would end in one generation.

Some scientists attempt to explain away the concept of irreducible complexity by claiming that elements of the body may have served other functions previously and therefore all the elements of the developing system may not have been originally present. This explanation doesn't explain, because the supposed incremental changes in the elements or parts of a working system would make the system no longer functional. The changes in the complete cell chemistry or bodily system would have to all change at the same time and immediately to continue to be functional. Otherwise death would result.

Non-functioning, partially developed systems would hinder the organism rather than assisting it. There is no time for these systems to slowly develop. The lack of any ingredient of these irreducible elements would have prevented their origination in the first place. German Information scientist & engineer, Werner Gitt summarizes this in "What Darwin Couldn't Know,"

"All conceivable evolutionary explanations fail miserably, because any partially completed transitional stage as evolution requires would not permit the organism to survive. The whole complex machinery is needed from the start."[358]

Evolution from simple to more complex life forms is supposed to work through natural selection. Science has proven, in contrast, that natural selection cannot create new information but only operates on the genetic information already there. Evolution requires additional information. As Hugo de Vries, Dutch Botanist said, *"Natural selection may explain the survival of the fittest, but it cannot explain the arrival of the fittest."*[359]

What this means is that change is within a limited scope using the information already in that genetic material. Without a way to increase information natural selection cannot be a vehicle for evolution. Evolutionists agree but assume that mutations create the necessary new information, which has been proven false in all mutations studied.

In Darwin's day it was thought the cell was quite simple. The reality is that every cell is very complex. The cell contains a miniature factory and is programmed with huge amounts of information. The ardent atheist Richard Dawkins, has acknowledged that a single celled amoeba contains more information than the entire <u>Encyclopedia Britannica</u>. A human cell contains even more.

The cell not only has this information stored but in cooperation with other elements in the cell, DNA processes the information to protect, repair and replicate itself.

Werner Gitt explains in his book, <u>In The Beginning Was Information</u> that matter and energy cannot create information. In a lecture Gitt quoted American Mathematician Norbert Weiner, who frequently stated that information cannot be a physical entity. *"Information is information, neither matter nor energy."*[360]

Information requires a mind. This is an evidence of God. Gitt continued, *"Because information is a non-material entity, its origin is likewise not explainable by material processes. ... Information always depends upon the will of the sender, who initially creates the information."*[361]

Gitt used the example of a computer chip – it is material but contains information that was placed in it by will and intelligence. He states, *"Information never exists on its own or of itself but must always have an intelligent source."*[362] **He informs us that irrational forces and chance cannot create information:** *"No merely chemical or physical process produced* *information" "There is no new information without an intelligence as a communicator or willful sender."*[363]

One of Gitt's conclusions is that: *"Since (1) biological information, the fundamental component of all life, originates only from an intelligent sender and (2) all theories of chemical and biological evolution require that information must have originated solely from matter and energy (no sender), we conclude that: All theories or concepts of chemical and biological evolution (macroevolution) are false."*[364]

Only intelligence, mind and will can create information. To program every living cell with these vast amounts of information and the ability to process that information requires a Supreme Intelligence.

The study of the human genes has been a fairly recent focus. The genes carry hereditary information and supervise the formation of proteins. Without the formation of proteins, our life would be impossible. The genetics professor Maciej Giertych of the Institute of Dendrology, the Polish Academy of Sciences said:

"We have become aware of the massive information contained in the genes. There is no way known to science how that information can arise spontaneously. It requires an intelligence. It cannot arise from chance events... complex DNA, RNA, protein replicating system in the cell must have been perfect from the very start. If not, life systems could not exist. The only logical explanation is that this vast quantity of information came from an intelligence."[365]

Molecular chemist Michael Behe, a former evolutionist, also discovered that complex structures like proteins cannot develop slowly over time. The elements of a protein must be complete, assembled simultaneously. In other words, the various elements necessary each require the existence of the other elements in order to form. If all the elements that make up that protein are not present at the same moment, the protein does not form at all.[366]

Michael Denton has gone into great detail to prove this is true and to show that the requirements to form protein molecules

and other characteristics of proteins indicate that macroevolution has not occurred.[367]

Denton introduces this information by first pointing out that until about 1960 the only way of classifying and assessing differences among species was based upon comparing structure. In other words, the biological assumption of evolution was actually based upon anatomy. The molecular biological revolution since then enables comparison of living organisms biochemically. The discovery was made that a particular protein sequence was not even the same between different species.[368] This has revealed the wide divergence between species rather than a close proximity based upon mere appearance.

Lack of Fossil Evidence

Darwin assumed the fossil record would support his theory as more fossils were discovered. Though we have far more fossils now, his assumption has not proven true. In fact scientists have assumed his theory to be correct and then interpreted the rock strata and fossils found in those strata so that they seemed to support the theory.[369] This is another evidence of evolutionists reasoning in a circle rather than providing actual evidence that supports the theory.

Evolutionists also assumed an ever expanding variety of life beginning from the single cell, to a widening cone with more and more life forms developing over time. However geologists working in Siberia, Canada and China, *"found at the beginning of the earth's Cambrian period, a biologic burst that produced almost all major groups of modern animals in an astonishingly short period of time."*[370]

Carl Wilson commenting on this writes, *"It is now clear that at least nine tenths of the forms and probably more that were thought non-existent already existed in most of the world by the time the first fossils were found in the rocks. ... This has never been the picture that evolutionists have presented."*[371]

Curator of the museum at Oxford University, **Tom Kemp** stated in <u>New Scientist:</u> *"As is now well known, most fossil* *species appear instantaneously in the fossil record, persist for some millions of years virtually unchanged, only to disappear abruptly."*[372]

These modern discoveries do agree however with a much earlier Introduction to Geology by Carl Branson W.A. Tarr and W.D. Keller, who in discussing early Cambrian life state: *"Probably nine-tenths of all basic organic structures in animals had appeared by the beginning of the Paleozoic period ..."*[373]

The cone is not as it was illustrated for Darwin's theory. In fact the fossil record shows that there are fewer life forms as time has gone on rather than more. Kurt Wise PHD in Paleontology from Harvard states,

"In the fossil record, however, such a 'cone of increasing diversity' is not observed. Instead, the number of major groups we have today was achieved early in earth's history, when species diversity was low. In fact, the number of classes of anthropods and echinoderms at the time of the first appearance of each of these groups was actually higher than it is at present."[374]

Michael Denton informs us that, *"An enormous effort has been made over the past century to find missing links in these rocks which might bridge the deep divisions in the animal kingdom. Yet no links have ever been found and the relationships of the major groups are as enigmatic today as one hundred years ago."*[375]

Denton quotes Norman Newall past curator in the American Museum of Natural History for historical geology: *"Many of the discontinuities tend to be more and more emphasized with increased collecting."*[376]

He is saying that the fossil record is not filling in gaps between various life forms to indicate continuity as evolution requires. Instead, the unique characteristics and separation of different species is becoming more pronounced, more obvious. This means that as more fossils have been found, the fossil record contradicts the theory of evolution even more than in the past.

Many organisms formerly unknown have been discovered in the past one hundred years. However, whether living or fossils these "*can in no way construed as connecting links in the sense required by evolution theory.*"[377]

Early in my undergraduate Geology textbook, it was stated that geologists dated the fossils by the rocks they were found in. Late in the text it was stated that the rocks were dated by the fossils found in them. The students were not supposed to notice this circular reasoning. The statements in the textbook proves that the theory is assumed true and the evidence is adjusted and placed as needed in order to appear to support the theory. That is not legitimate science.

As J.E. O'Rourke acknowledged in the <u>American Journal of Science:</u> "*The intelligent layman has long suspected circular reasoning in the use of rocks to date the fossils and fossils to date the rocks. The geologist has never bothered to think of a good reply, feeling the explanations are not worth the trouble as long as the work brings in the results.*"[378] So O'Rourke is acknowledging the deception of using circular reasoning and that as long as most people are fooled there is no reason to attempt to justify the deception.

The article, "Geology" in an earlier edition of the <u>Encyclopedia Britannica</u> confirmed this deceptive practice: "*It cannot be denied that from a strictly philosophical standpoint geologists are arguing in a circle. The succession of organisms has been determined by a study of their remains embedded in the rocks, and the relative ages of the rocks are determined by the remains of the organisms that they contain.*"[379]

In fact, according to Denton, "*In terms of their biochemistry, none of the species deemed 'intermediate', 'ancestral' or 'primitive' by generations of evolutionary biologists, and alluded to as evidence of sequence in nature, shows any sign of their supposed intermediate status.*"[380]

Evolutionists assume the needed sequence in nature to validate the theory and place the fossils where they are needed. They also rely on the basis of appearance and structural similarities, which to non-scientists seem convincing. However, biochemistry proves the relationships and sequences do not exist. More deception presented as science.

Evolutionists like to claim that similarities prove the theory, so let's compare blood. According to Professor H. Enoch, former Chair of the Department of Zoology at Madras University in India:

"Now it is true that some similarity exists between the blood of mammals which may even admit of their being arranged in a graded system. But this chemical similarity cannot prove evolution ... such inconvenient facts are ignored by evolutionists. Blood analysis has revealed other interesting facts. The specific gravity of human blood is 1059; for the pig and hare 1060 of frog 1055-56 of the snake 1055 and the monkey is 1054.9. From this table we can see that the frog and snake are closer to man than the monkey, while our nearest relation is the pig."[381]

That is a similarity based upon science that is completely ignored because it doesn't support the conclusions evolutionists wish us to make about origins.

Geneticist Maciej Giertych wrote that, *"As an academic teacher in population genetics I found it necessary to play down the evolutionary explanations given in textbooks, for the simple reason that I find no evidence to support them."*[382] **Giertych had been taught that paleontology was the source of most of the evidence for evolution but that,** *"To my surprise, I found that evidence is lacking not only in genetics but also in paleontology, as well as in sedimentology, in dating techniques, and in fact in all sciences."*[383]

Evolutionist Niles Eldridge admitted that *"We paleontologists have said that the history of life [in the fossil record] supports [the story of gradual adaptive change] ... all the while knowing that it does not."*[384]

Denton points out that it can no longer be claimed that there has been insufficient search or an incomplete fossil record as reason for the lack of support for evolution.[385]

Evolutionists needed some way to avoid the obvious conclusion that the fossil record disproves macroevolution.

In 1972, Niles Eldredge and Steven Jay Gould proposed the theory of punctuated equilibrium to solve this dilemma. This theory contends that stasis, or no change in the fossils was because for most of geological time the species remain the same. The theory went on to declare that evolution then would occur *"in brief episodes of branching speciation"*[386] (extensive change causing new forms of life to suddenly appear). Thus a way was found to claim that no evidence for evolution in the fossil record really was evidence after all!

In response to arguments that stasis or the lack of change was disproof of evolution, Gould wrote, *"On the contrary, stasis should be a positive conclusion based upon hard anatomical evidence of nonchange through substantial time."*[387]

Gould then adds, *"... stasis can provide only one side of the story, lest we be left with no evolution at all! The opposite and integrated side (the punctuation in punctuated equilibrium) proposes a concentration of change into relatively short episodes- jabs of reorganization in a world of generally stable systems."*[388]

Denton states that to consider this as the solution to the huge gaps such as exists between mammals and whales, or mollusks and arthropods would require belief in miracles (which he does not accept).[389] Darwin, himself agreed that assuming sudden transformation was to *"enter into the realm of miracle and leave those of science."*[390]

Giertych soon realized that *"Evolution is not a conclusion drawn from observations. It is an ideology to which observations are applied when convenient and ignored when not."*[391]

Many complex animals are now shown to have existed in the pre-Cambrian era where it had been assumed there were no living things. Most animal species are now known to have existed in the Cambrian era and mammals lived long before dinosaurs became extinct.[392]

The question to ask is, why did at least 90% of species not require an evolutionary process? Though discoveries are still couched in evolutionary terms, the theory is increasingly becoming scientifically contradictory and untenable. Despite great efforts to find missing links, the fossil record does not verify evolution.

A final nail in the coffin of macroevolution is the many discoveries of soft tissue in a variety of animal fossils. This proves they could not have been buried for millions of years.[393]

Evidence From Health Sciences

Beginning in the 1970's, research began to make it obvious that there was a positive correlation between religious commitment and mental health. This is completely contrary to Freud and most Psychiatrists and Psychotherapists prior to that time.[394] Sigmund Freud's perspective was avidly atheistic and he attacked religious belief continuously. *"Freud's view of religious belief shaped the majority outlook of the mental health profession, especially in the United States."*[395]

Freud's outlook has proven to be false and the opposite of what medical science has been discovering for the last four decades. Religious practices and faith in God are proving to have significant mental and physical health benefits.

Recently two Chinese researchers at Hong Kong Polytechnic University have reviewed dozens of studies and concluded that, contrary to Freud, the evidence is conclusive that strong positive religious faith enhances mental health.[396]

Senior researcher David Larson with the National Institute of Mental Health was interviewed in regard to the bias against religion in this field. He had surveyed psychiatric journals previously to compile evidence to verify the harmful effects of religion on health. He was surprised to discover the opposite. Over 80% of the journal's cases indicated benefits to the patients from religious practices.[397]

The effects of religion on health had been rarely studied in universities. This was because unless the study seemed to indicate religion was harmful to health, the subject was not considered academically acceptable. Larson found in his own study of men who enjoyed attending church that compared to non-attenders, the attenders had significantly lower blood pressure.[398]

An article in the December 1998 issue of McCall's magazine reported that Medical Doctors acknowledge that faith can boost the immune system, improve wellbeing and even prolong life.[399]

Even the liberal New York Times has taken notice. *"One of the most striking scientific discoveries about religion in recent years is that going to church weekly is good for you. Religious attendance – at least religiosity boosts the immune system and decreases blood pressure. It may add as much as two to three years to your life. The reason for this is not entirely clear."*[400]

The anthropologist reporting of his research in this article in the Times stated that wider social support through church connections and healthier lifestyles definitely contributed to these results, but more study is needed. He assumed that this was an example of the placebo effect. In other words, he didn't believe that God was real but that believing there is a loving God has a positive effect on health.[401]

Having religious or spiritual convictions as well as frequent attendance at religious services were both found to have positive benefits on one's mental and psychological well-being. Psychiatrist M. Scott Peck's book, The Road Less Traveled made a revolutionary impact on psychotherapy in 1978 with its case for God and spirituality.[402]

Peck wrote that, *"What I would now like to suggest is that it is also possible to mature into a belief in God. A skeptical atheism or agnosticism is not necessarily the highest state of understanding at which human beings can arrive. To the contrary, there is reason to believe that behind spurious notions and false concepts of God there lies a reality that is God."*[403]

There is now strong evidence for a correlation between spirituality and physical health as well. Harold G Koenig, M.D. is the founder and director of the widely respected Center for the Study of Religion/Spirituality and Health at Duke University. He and colleagues have carried out twenty five research projects since 1985 on the impact of faith, scripture reading and attendance at religious services upon health. He has written nearly 150 scientific articles as well as many books in this field.

Dr. Koenig writes, *"Over the years, other professional colleagues and I have scientifically documented a very definite and powerful faith health connection."*[404] **There is now a mountain of evidence that the mind and body were designed for worship and faith in God. Just to cite a few examples:**

- "People who frequently attended religious services had significantly more effective and stable immune systems.[405]

- "People who regularly attend church, pray and read religious scriptures have lower blood pressures and are less likely to have the disease hypertension.

- "People who attend church and pray or read religious scriptures regularly are less likely to abuse alcohol or smoke cigarettes.

- "People who attend church regularly live longer …

- "People who provide religious support and encouragement to others – through prayer, scripture reading etc. – experience greater quality of life and less depression when physically ill.

- Suicide rates are much less common among actively involved Christians.[406]

- "People who are actively involved in a religious community and those who have strong religious faith need and use fewer expensive health services.[407]

- Religiously involved persons have greater hope, are more optimistic, and have greater purpose and meaning.[408]

There are numerous studies by others of the impact of positive religious belief and practice. The vast majority of these studies confirm the beneficial results on physical and mental health. An exception is when the person cannot sense that God loves them, or that God is good.[409]

Another example is that utilizing data from The Women's Health Initiative. This study involving 95,000 women showed that of those over 59 years old, those who regularly attended services were 20% less likely to die in any year that those who never attended religious services.[410]

Dr. Stibich also felt part of the reason for this could be that certain religions promote healthier lifestyles and social connections. He reported another study that attendance at weekly religious services added 2-3 years of life to those participants.[411]

This supported earlier studies which reported monthly visits to church improved mental health of the elderly, and those attending weekly had lower levels of interleukin-6 which is associated with diseases related to aging. Actual attendance was also found to be more beneficial than merely tuning into religious broadcasts.[412]

There are also numerous studies showing a positive correlation between intercessory prayer and healing.[413] The results occur even when prayer is at a distance and the people being prayed for do not know they are being prayed for.[414]

Medical Doctor Larry Dorsey was first skeptical then uncomfortable with increasing awareness of this data. He realized, *"Experiments with people showed that prayer positively affected high blood pressure, wounds, heart attacks, headaches and anxiety."*[415]

Dorsey went on to say in regard to his findings about the efficacy of prayer that: *"I came to realize the truth of what many historians of science have described: A body of knowledge that does not fit with prevailing ideas can be ignored as if it does not exist, no matter how scientifically valid it may be."*[416]

The declaration that there is no God is a claim to know what cannot be shown; a claim that violates increasing evidence from various sciences. It is a claim that originates in false assumptions and bias rather than reality. The primary scientific foundation for atheism is found to be little more than smoke and mirrors. Despite all the presence and pressure to maintain the illusion that evolution is true, it no longer can be considered credible

Refuting Atheistic Propaganda

Sociologist Rodney Stark advocates neither evolution nor Intelligent Design. His book <u>For The Glory of God</u> **(2003), has given surprising evidence that Darwinists have hidden increasing flaws in the theory of evolution. He also shows that the battle over evolution is hardly the case of heroic scientists fighting off the persecution of religious fanatics as evolutionists pretend.**

Rather, from the start, evolutionists have militantly attacked and sought to refute all religious claims of a creator. In the process of their attacks they often attempted to suppress and silence any scientific evidence or criticism of Darwin's theory.[417] **They also attempt to discredit scientists and other scholars who present evidence and arguments contradicting the sacred cow of evolution. This was how they treated Behe, Velikovsky, Gentry, Giertych, Philip Johnson, and many others.**

Microbiologist Michael Denton states categorically, that Darwin's macro-evolutionary theory has not *"been validated by one single empirical discovery or scientific advance since 1859. Despite more than a century of intensive effort on the part of evolutionary biologists, the major objections raised by Darwin's critics such as Agassiz, Pictet, Bronn and Richard Owen have not been met."*[418]

These scholars contemporary with Darwin each rejected Darwin's speculations for scientific reasons and their arguments are still valid, never having been refuted.

Denton concludes his dissection of evolution with these remarks:

"The influence of evolutionary theory on fields far removed from biology is one of the most spectacular examples in history of how a highly speculative idea for which there is no really hard scientific evidence can come to fashion the thinking of a whole society and dominate the outlook of an age ... One might have expected that a theory of such cardinal importance, a theory that literally changed the world, would have been something more than metaphysics, something more than myth."[419]

Atheists Switching Definitions

In his textbook on critical thinking skills, <u>Attacking Faulty Reasoning</u>, the author T. Edward Damer asks, *"Who has the responsibility to provide an argument for a disputed claim?"* and then answers *"... one who makes a positive or negative claim about something has what is called the burden of proof. ...If the claimant is asked 'Why?' or 'How do you know that is true?' he or she is logically obligated to produce reasons in behalf of the claim."* Damer completes the point with, *"Neither should we allow others to get by without defending their opinions, especially about important or controversial issues."*[420]

Some modern atheists seek to evade this obligation and responsibility through dishonest tactics. They have learned through discussion or debate that they cannot verify their assertions regarding the non-existence of God and so have sought to redefine atheism. The redefinition basically denies asserting that God does not exist but that atheism, *"is simply the absence of belief in God; that atheism has no beliefs ... Thus since atheism asserts nothing and has no beliefs or world view, it needs to prove nothing."*[421]

The editor of <u>An Anthology of Atheism And Rationalism</u> Gordon Stein asserts: *"If the atheist is simply without God, then he is not asserting anything. On the other hand, the theist is asserting something (God) so the burden of proof is on him ... Atheism is without God. It does not assert no God. The atheist does not say there is no God."*[422]

This is a dishonest ploy to make it seem as if all responsibility to authenticate one's beliefs are up to those who assert belief in God. It is intended to allow the atheist to attack belief in God but to claim no responsibility to defend or validate his or her own position.

This 'definition' of atheism is also dishonest because throughout the <u>Anthology of Atheism and Rationalism</u> many beliefs are asserted and an obvious worldview is held. These beliefs include ethical relativism and materialism with no effort to verify those beliefs. This subtle change in definition is an effort to evade the reality that they cannot justify their denial of the existence of God nor their other assumptions. Such a definition also implies atheism to be a faith floating in space without any rational basis.

The problem atheists have created for themselves with this approach is explained by Morey: *"Atheists attempt this definition for only one reason: to allow themselves to bring in any ideas they wish without having to prove anything. But in so doing they have rendered atheism incapable of falsification or verification. And, if it is true, (as they claim when attacking theism) that a word or an idea is nonsense if it is not capable of falsification or verification, then atheism is nonsense and should be dismissed as meaningless."*[423]

The concept of falsification refers to the ability to test a given statement or claim by methods which could potentially disprove the hypothesis. In other words, using the atheist's own argument, if statements about atheism are incapable of being either proven or disproved, it is to be rejected as meaningless, ridiculous, and absurd.

If atheists were sincere in their claims of not having any beliefs in regard to God nor asserting anything about God, they would have no reason or basis for arguing against God's existence! That they still do argue and attack belief in God shows the dishonesty of those claims.

Responding to Atheists

Atheist's cannot validate their faith and frequently contradict their own requirements for evidence and logic when defending their theories. They accept lower standards of evidence for evolution that they would never accept in actual scientific projects. This increasing scientific knowledge is making it more and more difficult to justify rejecting belief in a supernatural Creator. How then are believers to react to and confront the growing tendency to deny God despite these facts?

Kerby Anderson suggested three essential responses: Christians must always be ready to give an answer for the hope that is in us with gentleness and reverence (1Peter 3:15); Believers must share the Gospel and trust in the power of the Holy Spirit to convict and convince those who hear it (Romans 1:16). Most important of all is that the quality of life lived by those who profess to know God must be such that it confirms the truth they advocate (1Peter 2:15).[424]

A positively transformed life is great evidence for the reality of God. This was revealed by the cartoon character, Charlie Brown, who is said to have exclaimed, *"Joy is the most infallible proof of the presence of God."*[425] (Acts 16:16-34). Respond to atheists with relevant information, a little scripture, love and a dose of humor.

Many of the recent generation think of themselves as atheists primarily because they have not been presented with any of the contrary evidence and thinking. Presentation of some of the information revealing the absurdity of atheism is sufficient to get many of these persons to reconsider their assumptions about science, reality and God.

Here is a summary of an approach used by J. Edwin Orr, a chaplain in the US Air Force during WW2. He began by asking pilots who claimed to be atheists, 'How much of total knowledge available to man do you actually know? Einstein said he knew about 2% of all available knowledge. Would it be fair to say you know about 1% if Einstein knew 2%?'

They usually agreed. Then he would ask, 'Would it be fair to say that God may exist in that other 99% of knowledge that you do not have?' Most of the pilots would admit it was theoretically possible. Chaplain Orr would respond, 'Then you are not an atheist; you're an agnostic.'

The term agnostic was still unfamiliar to most people back in the 1940's. Many pilots would ask, 'What's an agnostic?' Orr would explain that an agnostic is someone who states that they do not know if there is a God. Orr would then ask 'Are you an ordinary or an ornery agnostic?'

By this point some of the men were irritated. They asked Orr, 'What do you mean?' The chaplain's answer was that an ordinary agnostic merely admitted he did not know if there is a God, whereas an ornery agnostic declares, 'I don't know, you don't know, no one knows!' Orr continued, 'If you say that, I'm going to ask, if you don't know if there is a God, how do you know I don't know?'[426]

If someone admits they do not know if God exists, they cannot logically declare that no one else knows. Their admission of not knowing whether God exists, disqualifies them from knowing whether someone else might know.

Anthony Flew was mentioned earlier. He had often debated Christians arguing that there was no God. He declared that science had finally convinced him there had to be a God. He apparently became a Deist, one who believes in a creator but not a personal God who offers a relationship to us.

In his book describing the journey away from Atheism titled **There Is A God** Antony Flew wrote, "*I now believe that the universe was brought into being by an infinite Intelligence. I believe the universe's intricate laws manifest what scientists have called the Mind of God. I believe that life and reproduction originate in a divine Source.*"[427]

A reviewer of Flew's book said, *"What's noteworthy is that Flew came to these conclusions without any religious conversion ... He's just going on what he can figure out for himself. 'My discovery of the divine has been a pilgrimage of reason and not of faith,' he writes 'I have followed the argument to where it has led '"*[428] **Flew indicated abandoning atheism was not a quick decision but one that had been percolating in him for some time due to science.**

Earlier Einstein's reluctant admission that there had to be a creator was mentioned. Einstein later said: *"My religion consists of a humble admiration of the illimitable superior spirit who reveals himself in the slight detail we are able to perceive with our frail and feeble minds. That deeply emotional conviction of the presence of a superior reasoning power, which is revealed in the incomprehensible universe, forms my idea of God."*[429]

Why would a scientist or anyone else be reluctant to follow the evidence wherever it leads? Why are the unverifiable theories of macroevolution and atheism often taught as if they were scientific facts despite the evidence against both? The primary explanation is, these theories are preferred by their advocates to the alternative of a Creator. The theories are preferred because truth is often inconvenient and uncomfortable. Truth often demolishes human pride, exposes ulterior motives and does not lead where one has already chosen to go.

As referenced earlier, Cyril Joad spent his career as a philosophy professor dedicated to destroying Christianity. After his conversion to Christ he wrote, *"There is such a thing as pride of the intellect, a pride in which throughout my life I have been continuously proud."*[430] **He further stated that the pride of intellect was the major reason modern intellectuals find it difficult to believe in God.**

In <u>Ideas Have Consequences</u>, Richard Weaver explained the increasing favor of atheism. *"The modern position seems only another manifestation of egoism, which develops when man has reached a point at which he will no longer admit the right to existence of things not of his own contriving."*[431] **Weaver added,**

"For modern man there is no providence, because it would imply a wisdom superior to his ..."[432] *"...man is not making himself like a god but is taking himself as he is and putting himself in the place of God. Of this we have seen many instances."*[433]

Summary Of The Evidence

This presentation has shown that, reason, human experience, history, arguments for and against God's existence, as well as scientific facts; all indicate that theism (belief in a personal God) is more reasonable then atheism. Atheism is lacking any authentic scientific support, and contradicts fundamental scientific facts as well as reason.

There is extensive and growing scientific evidence indicating a Creator and contradicting the theory of macroevolution. Unfortunately, those desiring to eliminate the evidence for a Creator are often in a position to use both censorship and indoctrination through the media and in the schools to make their preferences seem true. Withholding and misinterpretation of scientific information along with the fabrication of apparent explanations gives the illusion that evolution is factual. These tactics provide the fraudulent appearance of a scientific foundation for atheism.[434]

By these methods, people are misled into thinking that evolution and atheism are based upon science and belief in God is based upon faith. In reality evolution and atheism are based upon faith that contradicts history, science and reason.

Atheism has to assume by a gigantic leap of faith that somehow nothing at all was able to create everything, or to ignore science completely and assume the universe is eternal. Another huge leap of faith is that non-living matter gave birth to living things, to consciousness and to rational thought. To believe that somehow nonliving and living matter has become more and more complex despite the laws of physics is blind faith.

It is faith that claims natural selection produces advances in the complexity of biological life. This faith contradicts scientific knowledge by assuming accumulated mutations cause an advance to more complex life. Mutations result in a loss of information in the cell, rather than the increase in information macroevolution requires.

Another leap of faith is to assume that the increasing evidence of design is the result of blind chance and random processes. Assuming that matter and energy can produce information is irrational faith. Information always originates from a mind. It is also faith that decrees that the nearly universal belief in God is merely ignorance and superstition. Atheism is upheld by many individual leaps of faith that contradict reality and reason.

The world religions teach many conflicting ideas about God and reality. They cannot all be true. The Bible and the Christian faith do not merely advocate that everyone should believe in some general concept of a God. Nor do they promote the idea that some vague acknowledgement that God exists is what matters.[435] The biblical perspective is that God wants and invites us into relationship with Himself.

There are many publications presenting evidence that the Christian Faith is unique among all the alternatives available.[436] There is sufficient evidence for those willing to follow the evidence, that these unique features show the Christian faith must have its origin in the Creator. This book is based upon the premise that if one is committed to follow the evidence all the way to its ultimate conclusion, one will discover that God has revealed Himself through creation, through our intuition, through the biblical prophets, and supremely through Jesus Christ.[437]

Constancio Amen, a philosophy instructor stated that *"Jesus is Unique in history."* **He went on to write that:**

"The issue of God's existence turns on Jesus of Nazareth in this way: if the claims He made are true, then the question of God's existence has been settled. ... So the greatest question of history is: Who was Jesus of Nazareth? ... How many of those who deny the claims of Jesus have open-mindedly studied the account of

Jesus deeds and His claims? ... in most cases the rejection of the claims of Jesus has been arrived at within the confines of ignorance ... The fair minded man will not come to a conclusion concerning an issue of history without carefully considering the pertinent data; to do so is to be dogmatic, hence unscientific.'[438]

The data he referred to is primarily in the New Testament documents, especially the Gospels.

One reason atheism seems so acceptable to Western thinking despite the growing scientific evidence refuting it, is that secular humanism has been the dominant worldview promoted in our universities and scientific journals for over 150 years. The constant repetition of the absurdity of atheism can create the illusion of credibility and cause many to embrace it, at least temporarily.

Some Former Atheists

Following are a few of the former atheists who investigated the facts, followed the evidence all the way and rejected atheism for the Christian faith:

Lew Wallace, lawyer, Civil War General, politician and author, did research to disprove the information about Jesus. He was converted and wrote the most famous novel ever about Christ, <u>Ben Hur</u>. Through that book he sought to draw others to faith. His book has been a best seller since its publication in 1880.

G.K. Chesterton was a prominent English Journalist, philosopher and literary figure of the early 20th century. His conversion from atheism and writings, especially <u>The Everlasting Man</u> and <u>Orthodoxy</u> were significant influences in bringing former atheist C.S. Lewis to the Christian faith.

Emile Cailliet, French intellectual compiled quotes, insights, experiences etc. that was to be the book that would understand him. When he felt the book was complete he began to read it. He found it merely reminded him of the situations in which he had gained the information, or insight. Meanwhile his wife had obtained a Bible, a forbidden book in

their home. When Emile arrived home she began to apologize. He said, *"A Bible? Let me have it, I've never seen one."* Reading for hours, he realized this was the book that understood him and was converted.[439]

C.S. Lewis, Cambridge University professor, wrote the autobiographical <u>Surprised By Joy</u>. He tells of his reluctant conversion first to Theism and then to Christ. As a result, he also wrote numerous books defending Christianity including <u>Mere Christianity</u>, <u>Miracles</u>, <u>The Problem of Pain</u>, <u>The Abolition of Man</u> and <u>Christian Reflections</u>.[440]

Cyril Joad, past Director of the School of Philosophy at London University, had spent his career trying to destroy the Christian faith. He finally wrote a book titled <u>Recovery of Belief</u>. He said two world wars and the prospect of a third had finally convinced him that man was not basically good; that human evil was a reality. Since only the Bible had a genuine solution to evil, he had become a Christian.[441]

Dr. Gerhard Dirks, Hitler's top electronics expert immigrated to the U.S. He developed some of the earliest memory systems for computers. With an IQ estimated at 208, he had always considered the Bible to be for inferior minds. While recuperating from an ailment he spent two weeks studying and analyzing the New Testament. He said he could not refute the evidence that Jesus Christ was God and so he committed his life to Christ.

Ignace Lepp, This French Psychoanalyst and former Marxist became disillusioned. Later he began to question the meaning of life. He thought it illogical that beings able to think and love could be in an absurd universe with nothing to think, love or hope. In this frame of mind he encountered the Christian message and became a believer.[442]

Josh McDowell thought Christians were out of their minds and decided to do the research to prove that. <u>Skeptic's Quest</u> tells of his research convincing him that Christianity was true. He has since written many books presenting evidence for the Christian faith.[443]

Boris Dotsenko. This former top-ranking Soviet physicist, one-time Director of Nuclear Physics, Institute of Physics, Kiev, Ukraine. He mentions having been a thoroughly convinced atheist. Contemplating the second law of thermodynamics he realized that science itself required a powerful Creator to sustain the universe.

Reading the Gideon Bible in his hotel room he was converted to the Christian faith. *"Disillusionment with the ideology of materialistic Communism,"* **says Dr. Denseko,** *"is that common factor in the lives of Soviet intellectuals who are finding God."* [444] *"I believe that God is the Creator of the universe, but He is not confined to it."* [445]

Sergie Golovin, a former Soviet Geo-physicist. For a scientific expedition, he was the only one of his team to receive the exit permit from the USSR. At his assignment on Spitzbergen Island Golovin was handed a Bible by a Norwegian pastor. Golovin had been indoctrinated in atheism, but having nothing to do at night, he decided to see what this book of fairy tales was like. Reading the Bible brought him to faith in Jesus Christ.

Speaking about Soviet Society, Golovin stated *"Three generations of communist 'atheology' has trained people not to search for a logical answer. The logical contradictions in communist ideology were carefully explained away as just the dialectic of history. So even if they see contradictions in parts of evolution theory many still accept it."*[446]

Lee Strobel was legal editor and a trained research reporter for the Chicago Tribune. His research to disprove Christianity, after his wife's conversion, led him to Christ. *"The facts of science systematically eroded the foundation of Darwinism until it could no longer support the weight of my atheistic conclusions."*[447] **He has since written <u>Evidence For Faith</u>, <u>Evidence for Christ</u> and <u>Evidence For A Creator</u>.**

Patrick Glynn, Associate Director of the George Washington University Institute for Communitarian Policy Studies wrote a very significant book titled, <u>God: The Evidence</u>. The first chapter is titled, "The Making and Unmaking of an Atheist." The book presents the information that turned him away from atheism. He wrote "*I finally realized that there was in fact a God.*"[448]

Former atheist Alister McGrath, Professor of Historical Theology at Oxford University, possesses Doctorates in Molecular Biophysics and Theology. He wrote <u>The Dawkins Delusion?</u> to contradict some of the flaws in Richard Dawkins <u>The God Delusion</u>. He also wrote <u>The Twilight Of Atheism</u>.

This is a sampling of those who have been willing to reassess their presuppositions in light of the evidence. They traded the unscientific and unproven assumptions of atheism for the reality of God.

I hope this presentation will cause you to evaluate your presuppositions and world view sufficiently to genuinely consider not only the likelihood of God's existence but also the possibility of a relationship with Him. Read further evidence for God presented in some of the writings listed in the Bibliography.

It should be obvious by now that the atheist's worldview requires faith even more than does belief in God. The difference is that belief in God has solid scientific evidence and reason to back it up. The faith of atheism, in contrast, is mainly a game of avoidance, denial and distortion of facts, conjecture, making up rules they refuse to abide by themselves, as well as emotional and illogical arguments.

Concluding Statements

Dr. James H. Shaw, associate professor of biological chemistry at Harvard School of Dental Medicine comments, "*... no satisfaction for the yearning human heart can spring from any amoral, impersonal body of knowledge. Science has no answer to man's dilemma.*"[449]

Dr. Raymond Damadian, cited earlier, states that, "*... for the scientific mind, the Bible is wonderful if you read it from start to* *finish. It fits together with an astonishing consistency, which was the opposite of my secular perception."*[450]

Malcolm Dixon, is a British scientist whose work is in enzyme biochemistry. He obtained two doctorates at Cambridge. He declared: *"For over forty years I have been engaged in scientific research and teaching at the advanced level in Cambridge University, and have found no reason to think there is any incompatibility between science and Christianity. Many of the greatest scientists have been Christian ..."*[451]

Distinguished professor of Physics at Texas A & M University, Dr. John A. McIntyre, emphasizes that,

"The general opinion seems to be that science has replaced religion as the source of answers for human questions so that religious ignorance is to be encouraged ... As a scientist who discovered the Christian message as an adult, I can testify to the profundity and appeal of the Christian explanation of these facts: that man is estranged from God and that his life is empty and incomplete until he returns to God through his son, Jesus Christ. Further, I know of no scientific facts which contradict this view."[452]

After presenting the biblical perspective of reality and interaction with a group of Russian generals at the Center for Geopolitical Strategy in Moscow, the ranking general, said, *"Dr. Zacharias, I believe what you have brought us is the truth. But it is so hard to change after seventy years of believing a lie.***"**[453]
The General is correct!

Resource Endnotes

[1] Georges P/ Carillet. "Symposium on 'Christianity, Humanism, Health' an Introduction." Truth and Consequences, 2006. p.155.
[2] T. Edward Damer. Attacking Faulty Reasoning. Wadsworth Publishing, 3rd. ed., 1995. p. 16.
[3] Roger Baker. "If We Covered the U.S. Election." Strathor Geopolitical Weekly, April 26, 2016.
[4] Georges P. Carillet. "Symposium on 'Christianity, Humanism, Health' an Introduction." p. 156.
[5] Calvin Miller. A Thirst For Meaning. Zondervan Publishing House, 1973. p. 16.
[6] Paudge Mulinhill. "From Atheism To Christ." Ireland's 4You Magazine. Issue XI. p. 13.
[7] John Blanchard. Is Anybody Out There? Evangelical Press, 2006. p. 4.
[8] Katherine Hayhoe. "The Roots of Science Denial." Scientific American. October 2017. p. 66.
[9] Cyril Joad. Recovery of Belief. Faber and Faber Limited, 1952. p. 28.
[10] Ibid. Joad presents the intellectual basis for his departure from atheism and embracing the Christian faith.
[11] Alister McGrath. The Dawkins Delusion. Inter-Varsity Press, 2007. p. 23.
[12] Sam Harris. The End of Faith. W.W. Norton, 2005. p. 17.
[13] Ravi Zacharias. The Real Face of Atheism. Baker Books, 2004. p. 19.
[14] Richard Dawkins. The God Delusion. Houghton Mifflin, 2006. p. 35.
[15] Josh McDowell & Don Stewart. Understanding Secular Religions. Here's Life Publishers, 1982. p. 14.
[16] Clive Staples Lewis. Mere Christianity. The Macmillan Company, 1960. p. 29.
[17] Deism." DK Illustrated Oxford Dictionary. Dorling Kindersley Limited and Oxford University Press, Inc. 1998. p. 217.
[18] "Deism." Collins/Cobuild Advanced Dictionary of American English. p. 335. "Deism is the belief that there is a God who made the world, but does not influence human lives.
[19] Alister McGrath. The Twilight of Atheism. Doubleday, 2004. p. 8.
[20] Ibid. pp. 5-7.
[21] Ignace Lepp. Atheism In Our Time. Macmillan Company, 1963. pp. 10-11.
[22] Alister McGrath. The Twilight of Atheism. pp. 8-9. Also <en.wikepedia.org/wiki/atheism>. Referencing Michael Martin (ed.). The Cambridge Companion to Atheism. Cambridge University Press, 2006.
[23] <en.wikipedia.org/wiki/atheism>. Citing Karen Armstrong. A History of God. Vintage Books, 1999.
[24] Alister McGrath. The Twilight of Atheism. pp. 10-11.
[25] Ibid.
[26] Ibid, p. 10.
[27] Ibid. p. 11.
[28] Ibid.

[29] Robert A. Morey. The New Atheism and the Erosion of Freedom. Presbyterian & Reformed Publishing, 1986. pp. 38-39.
[30] James I. Packer. "Atheism." Inter-Varsity Magazine. Intro. Issue, 1864. p. 4.
[31] A massive amount of evidence has been accumulated by anthropologists verifying that monotheism was the original religion of mankind. That research has never been refuted but is usually ignored or denied. See the work of Andrew Lang, Myth, Ritual And Religion, and Wilhelm P. Schmidt, The Origin and Growth of Religion. In The Origin of Religion by Samuel Zwemer, there are references to the work of others supplementing and confirming Lang and Schmidt. Judaism and Christianity then are a restoration and extension of that original knowledge of God. See my 2013 publication, The Uniqueness of the Christian Faith. That book demonstrates that the historic biblical Christian Faith is radically different from the world religions, and has marks of Divine origin missing in all those religions. If then Christianity is true, the religions are all false, including atheism.
[32] Ignace Lepp. Atheism In Our Time. pp. 11-12.
[33] Ibid. p. 12.
[34] James I. Packer. "Atheism." pp. 4-5.
[35] Ibid.
[36] <en.wkipedia.org/wiki/atheism> "Worldwide Adherents of All Religions by Six Continental Areas" Encyclopedia Britannica, 2005. The article specified 2.3% as atheists, but another 11.9 % as non-religious – many of whom should be categorized as atheists. A global poll by WIN/GIA in 2012 indicated 13% of humanity describe themselves as atheists. "Religiosity and Atheism Index," Zurich WIN/GIA, July 27, 2012. We find that a Christian, a Deist, and others may define the term 'atheist' differently than each other. Another difficulty is that surveys ask different questions and questions phrased in different ways in order to come up with their percentages.
[37] <en.wikipedia.org/wiki/atheism>. "Religious Views and Beliefs Vary Greatly By Country, According To the Latest Financial Times/Harris Poll." Financial Times/Harris Interactive. 20 December 2006.
[38] Christianity Today. "The New Intolerance. February, 2007. p. 24.
[39] Ignace Lepp. Atheism In Our Time. p. 11.
[40] Ibid. p. 12.
[41] Ibid. p. 8.
[42] Ibid. p. 95, 119, 121, 138.
[43] <http://plato.stanford.edu/entries/ludwig-feuerbach/>.Published Dec. 9, 2013.
[44] Robert A. Morey. The New Atheism. p. 39.
[45] Ignace Lepp. Atheism In Our Time. pp. 132-133.
[46] Ignace Lepp. Atheism In Our Time. pp. 120-123. Sartre, however does not see this absolute freedom as a blessing or good thing but a curse, because to him, everything is absurd, therefore there is no meaning or benefit even to man's freedom.
[47] Ibid. p. 9.
[48] Ibid. pp. 7-8.

[49] *"The concept of organic evolution is very highly prized by biologists, for many of whom it is an object of genuinely religious devotion ...'* Evolutionist E. G. Conkin <u>Man, Real and Ideal</u>. Scribner, 1943. p. 147. *"Neo-Darwinism has already showed signs of hardening into quasi-religious dogma ..."* Darwinist Nigel Calder. Nature255, 1975. p. 8. Both cited by British Physicist Alan Hayward. <u>Creation and Evolution</u>. Bethany House, 1985. p. 16.

[50] Steven Kostoff. "If There is No God--Then Everything Is Permitted." <provmir.com/article_678.html> July 22, 2009.

[51] Robert A. Brace. "Secularism – The Most Evil Philosophy Known to Human Government." <Ukapologetics.net/09/secularism> 2nd ed., 2008.

[52] Robert A. Morey. <u>The New Atheism: And the Erosion of Freedom</u>. pp. 28-29.

[53] Elizabeth Pennisi. "Hackel's Embryos: Fraud Rediscovered." <u>Science Magazine</u>. Vol. 277, No. 5331. Sept 5, 1997. p. 1435. <Sciencemag.org> "Using modern techniques, a British researcher has photographed embryos like those pictured in the famous, century-old drawings by Ernst Haeckel--proving that Haeckel's images were falsified. Haeckel once admitted to his peers that he doctored the drawings, but that confession was forgotten."

[54] Jonathan Wells. <u>Icons of Evolution: Science or Myth?</u> Regnery Publishing, 2000. pp. 209-228. The pretense of knowing a series of steps from ape to man is another example of circular reasoning. The theory is assumed to be true, then any related evidence is interpreted as would be consistent were the theory true, then it is claimed to validate the theory. This assumed sequence of human evolution was formulated before there were any human fossil remains which proves biased and deceptive intentions. The remains as they are found are plugged into the assumed linage as fits the theory. The reconstructions, often largely guesswork, or fabricated are shown in drawings that appear to show a progression from apes or chimps to humans. These are then presented as "proof." These "reconstructions" are arbitrary, can vary enormously and are misleading as some evolutionists admit.

[55] Jonathan Wells. <u>Icons of Evolution</u>. Regnery Publishing, 2000. pp. 126-129. *"Brian Cooley, who specializes in in reconstructing dinosaurs from fossil skeletons ... explained to the participants that he <u>set out to make Bambiraptor as</u> <u>bird-like as possible</u>, given its <u>supposed</u> position between dinosaurs and birds. He reconstructed the muscles using bird anatomy as his guide, and he placed the eyes in a bird-like orientation... <u>Guessing</u> that Bambiraptor <u>must have been</u> covered with 'scruffy' feathers, Colley <u>added them</u> to his reconstruction."*

[56] The Scopes trial in Dayton, Tennessee pitted evolution against creation. An alleged "Nebraska man," was the evidence presented for evolution. This was assumed to a missing link between humans and apes. The only support for this "link" was a single tooth which later (after the trial) was proven to be from an extinct peccary, a member of the pig family.

[57] Vestigial organs are organs in humans that, according to evolutionists, served in earlier stages of evolution but were no longer necessary, though still present in humans. There was once about 100 of these asserted leftovers from our assumed evolution. They are now all known to serve important functions for humans. The last ones to be designated as vestigial were the appendix and the tailbone. As it turns out even these have functions in humans though some textbooks still have not been updated in this regard. The importance of all these organs was merely unknown in earlier stages of the sciences of human anatomy and physiology.

[58] Jonathan Wells. Icons of Evolution. pp. 123-124, 217-219. Reference to the Piltdown Man hoax which involved a fake fossil supposedly dug up at Piltdown in England in 1912. The fraud was not exposed until 1953.

[59] <scientificamerican.com/article/how-fake-fossils-pervert-paleontology-excerpt>

[60] Robert A. Morey. The New Atheism. p. 34-35. Gerald Stiles. "Bigotry in the Classroom?" Interest Magazine. January, 1982. p. 10.

[61] William A. Dembski. Intelligent Design. Inter-Varsity Press, 1999. p. 112.

[62] Robert A. Morey. The New Atheism. p. 34.

[63] Peter T. Chattaway. "The Chronicles of Atheism." Christianity Today, December, 2007. p. 37.

[64] The following is a small sampling of scientists outside the U.S. who each rejects or doubts the validity of evolution: John Polkinhhorne is a British Biophysicist; Maciej Giertych is a Polish Geneticist; Warner Gitt is a German Information scientist & engineer; Boris Dotsenko, is a Ukrainian Atomic Physicist; Sergie Golovin is a former Soviet Geophysicist, just one of several Russian Scientists who have rejected or doubt the validity of evolution. Two Japanese Biologists Kiruma and Ohta were criticized in Nature for daring to express criticism of evolution. Michael Dention, the Australian Microbiologist, states that opposition to evolution has been greater in Europe than the U.S. See his Evolution: A theory in Crisis. p. 86. Denton's book effectively destroys any scientific basis for accepting macroevolution.

[65] Milton Steinberg. The Anatomy of Faith. Harcourt Brace, 1960. pp. 88-96. Cited by Dennis Prager & Joseph Telushkin. The Nine Questions People Ask About Judaism. p. 28.

[66] Robert A. Morey. The New Atheism: p. 34.

[67] Ibid. p. 35.

[68] James I Packer. "Atheism." p. 4.

[69] Ravi Zacharias. The Real Face of Atheism. Baker Books, rev. 2004. p. 25. Referencing Paul Johnson. Modern Times. Harper-Collins, rev. 2000.

[70] Ravi Zacharias. The Real Face of Atheism. pp. 26-27.

[71] Ibid. pp. 27-29.

[72] Alister McGrath. The Twilight of Atheism. p. 262.

[73] C.S. Lewis. "Lilies That Fester." The Worlds Last Night and Other Essays. Harcourt Brace Jovanovich. n.d. p. 40. *"The loftier the pretensions of power, the more meddlesome inhuman, and oppressive it will be."*

[74] Ravi Zacharias. The Real Face of Atheism. pp. 29-30.

[75] Sam Harris. The End of Faith. p. 12.

[76] The political motivation behind wars includes the Muslim conquests and internal struggles over the past 1400 years, The Crusades, the Protestant-Catholic battles in Northern Ireland and current Muslim violence in the West. Religion is an element yet the effort to gain political control is primary. There is no separation between the political and religion in Islam. The Catholics in Northern Ireland are Irish and the Protestants are British. The IRA were attempting to throw off British rule.

[77] It has been estimated that at least 100 million people were murdered by their own atheistic governments in Russia, Eastern Europe, China, Cambodia and North Korea. This is more than five times the number killed in World War II, which was also begun in Europe by the atheistic Nazi government.

[78] Robert Conquest. The Harvest of Sorrow. Oxford, 1986. pp. 301-307. Cited by Robert A. Brace. "Secularization – The Most Evil Philosophy Known to Human Government." Printout p. 3.

[79] Robert A. Brace. "Secularization – The Most Evil Philosophy Known to Human Government." printout p. 2. These figures reportedly agreed with those found in the papers of long-time Soviet Premier Anastas Mikoyan. Estimates of the dead due to the entire Soviet rule of Russia are 50 to 60 million.

[80] Ravi Zacharias. The Real Face of Atheism. pp. 30-33.

[81] Alister McGrath. The Twilight of Atheism. pp. 219.

[82] Ibid. p. 262.

[83] Richard M. Weaver. Ideas Have Consequences. University of Chicago Press, 1948. p. 99.

[84] Ibid.

[85] Barry Yeoman. "Schweitzer's Dangerous Discovery" Discover Magazine, April 2006. This is considered 'dangerous' because it is well-known soft tissue deteriorates within a few thousand years (at most). Helen Fields. "Dinosaur Shocker." Smithsonian magazine. May, 2006. Tracy Wilson. "How Did Scientists Find Soft Tissue in Dinosaur Bones?" <science.howstuffworks.com>. The first claim was that the sample had been contaminated. As more and more finds of soft tissue in fossils are coming to light it is being claimed that iron in the soft tissues preserved them. It may be that in the future to avoid the obvious contradiction with evolutionary theory atheistic scientists will pretend they have always "known" that soft tissue could survive for millions of years. Finds around the world have been recently reported in Science, Nature, Journal of Applied Genetics, Journal of Vertebrate Paleontology, Journal of the American Chemical Society etc. See <kgov.com/dinosaurs-softtissue#research>.

[86] Brian Thomas. "Dinosaurs and Dragon Legends." Acts & Facts. Institute for Creation Research. July 2017. pp. 114-116. The article quotes from some first century A.D. historians and other regarding creatures that sound very much like some dinosaurs. Also ancient depictions of dinosaurs have their legs coming straight down from their body as the fossils we have do. The reptiles we are familiar with today have legs that extend from the sides of their body and then bend at the knee or elbow on down to the ground.

[87] Bill Cote. "The Mysterious Origin of Man," The NBC Documentary first aired Feb. 25, 1996. It stated among other important facts that many scientific discoveries were hidden away from the public because they conflicted with current theories. We are finding out that is very true. Cave paintings and rock carvings of obvious dinosaurs have been described by these scientists as 'mythological creatures to hide their true identity. Ancient carvings and paintings of known Identifiable dinosaurs have been found in the U.S, Mexico, Peru, and Anchor Watt, Cambodia. For extensive photos see <bing.com/images/search?=dinosaurs+and+men>. Also footprints of humans along with those of dinosaurs in Texas, and Mexico. Even the National Center for Science Education published a report indicating apparent human footprints along with Dinosaurs found in 1986 in Turkmenia (a Former Soviet Republic). Also see: <bcvideo.com> & Dennis Swift. Secrets of the Ica Stones and Nazcal Lines. Self Published, 2006.

[88] Orlo Strunk Jr. The Choice Called Atheism. Abingdon Press, 1968. p. 8.

[89] Ibid.

[90] James I. Packer. "Atheism." pp. 5-6.

[91] Hugh Ross. Why The Universe Is the Way It Is. Baker Books, 2008. p. 104. This physicist and former atheist explains that without God nothing can reverse the decay of the universe and eventual extinction of all life here. Without God nothing would have any ultimate meaning or significance. See pp. 103-105.

[92] Francis Schaeffer. Death In the City. Inter-Varsity Press, 1969. p. 13.

[93] Ignace Lepp. Atheism In Our Time. p. 14.

[94] Calvin Miller. A Thirst For Meaning. Zondervan Publishing House, 1973. p. 15.

[95] Roy Abraham Varghese. "Preface" in Antony Flew. There Is A God. Harper Collins, 2007. pp. xvi-xvii.

[96] Stephen Pincock. "Three Great Origin Questions –Universe, Life Consciousness." Financial Times. Nov. 15, 2013.

[97] Examples of the flaws in logical positivism were: (1). That the foundational statement (worded differently in the next endnote below) required multiple assumptions that could not be verified. (2). That logical positivism is meaningless because the claim that meaning can only be ascertained by experiential proof fails its own test; the statement has no possibility of experiential proof.

[98] <www.brittanica.com> Encyclopedia Britannica. "Logical Positivism." Logical positivism was essentially the philosophy that the only kind of factual knowledge was scientific knowledge and all metaphysical beliefs were meaningless. There are other sources or methods of obtaining factual knowledge such as experience, intuition, reasoning and authority. Knowledge obtained from each of these areas must be carefully evaluated because of the possibility of error just as science is continually revised in light of further advances and discoveries. Many "facts" of science from 100 years ago are completely refuted today. Examples of refuted scientific beliefs are that the universe is eternal and that life can spontaneously arise from non-life.

[99] Roy Abraham Varghese. "Preface" in Antony Flew. There Is A God. pp. xvii-xviii.

[100] Tom Bothell. "What Is the World Really Like?" <u>Evolution News and Views</u>, September 14, 2013. Tom Bothell, famous investigative reporter and Editor did an extensive study of the alleged evidence for evolution. He recently wrote "In between the Creationists and Materialists we encounter the scientific evidence that makes the materialists position increasingly improbable --the evidence that Stephen Meyer recently presented in <u>Darwin's Doubt</u>: information theory, insufficiency of the fossil record, epigenetics, complexity of life at the molecular level, and so on." Bothell continued "Increasingly, it seems to me, the Darwinians are responding to this science by saying (in effect): 'Bah! We won't read that! Its creationism in disguise.'" They prefer to deny science that contradicts their faith in Darwin.

[101] Roy Abraham Varghese. "Preface" in Antony Flew. <u>There Is A God</u>. p. viii.

[102] Primary examples of atheists that want to see Christianity destroyed are: Sam Harris. <u>Letter To A Christian Nation</u>; Richard Dawkins. <u>The God Delusion</u>; Christopher. Hitchens. <u>God Is Not Great</u>.

[103] <u>USA Today</u> 1/30/2006 Reported the basis of Luigi Casioli's suit against the priest, Enrico Righi was that he had violated the Italian laws that forbids deceiving the public and forbids impersonation for financial gain. <u>The American Humanist Association</u> had earlier reported (July 5, 2004) that the Appeals Court in Rome had thrown the suit out and fined the atheist for filing a fraudulent suit. The author asked "Is this a just response to a misuse of legal procedure or an attempt to stifle atheist activism?" Obviously it was a misuse of legal procedure as there is more than sufficient evidence verifying Jesus as an historical person. The article does not consider the information available.

[104] Luigi Casioli, author of <u>The Fable of Christ</u>, appealed the court's decision and on the anniversary of the first suit filed a second in 2008. See previous note and: <luigicasioli.eu/traduzion/en_1.htm> <sidneyrigdon.com/vern/2001casioli.htm>

[105] First of all, the New Testament writings themselves are historical documents that must be accounted for. What adequately explains their origin? Some of the writers were eyewitnesses of the events they recorded. Others had access to eyewitnesses. Then we have the references to Jesus by the Greek Historian Thallus writing possibly as early as 52 AD, the Roman writers in the early second century: historians, Tacitus in his <u>Annals</u> XI, 44; Seutonius in <u>Lives of the Caesars</u>; Pliny, the Regional Government official writing to the emperor, "Letter of Pliny To Trajan." Lucian, the satirist writing later in the second century, <u>The Passing of Peregruis</u>. The Jewish (Babylonian) Talmud includes two references to Jesus. Details of these and other early non-biblical references are found in many places. One of the most thorough documentations is Josh McDowell's <u>He Walked Among Us: Evidence For the Historical Jesus</u>. Here's Life Publishers, 1988.

[106] Paul Johnson. <u>Jesus</u>. Penguin Books, 2010. p. 3.

[107] Walter Isaacson. "Einstein & Faith." <u>Time Magazine</u>, April 16, 2007. p. 46. An excerpt from the book <u>Einstein</u> by Isaacson prior to publication.

[108] Robert A. Morey. <u>The New Atheism And the Erosion of Freedom</u>. p. 27.

[109] Robert A. Morey. <u>The New Atheism</u>. p. 27. Madalyn O'Hair had sought to convince atheists as well as everyone else to stay away from the Bible.

[110] C.S. Lewis. Surprised By Joy: The Shape of My Early Life. Fontana Books, 1959. p. 180.
[111] "The New Intolerance: Fear Mongering among elite atheists is not a pretty sight." Christianity Today, February, 2007. p. 24.
[112] Ibid.
[113] Ibid.
[114] Michael Novak. "Remembering the Secular Age." First Things, June-July 2007. Cited by Paul Copan, Is God A Moral Monster? Making Sense of the Old Testament God. Baker Books, 2011. p. 17.
[115] Richard Dawkins. The God Delusion. Houghton Mifflin, 2006. p.74.
[116] John Blanchard. Is Anybody Out There? Evangelical Press, 2006. p. 8.
[117] Richard Dawkins. What We Believe But Cannot Prove. (ed.) John Brockman, Pocket Books, 2005. p. 9. Cited by Varghese, "Preface" to Antony Flew. There Is A God. p. xix.
[118] Richard Dawkins. The God Delusion. pp. 186, 188.
[119] Hugh Ross. Why The Universe Is The Way It Is. Baker Books, 2008. p. 132. "Everything restricted to the cosmic time line must be traceable back to a cause and beginning. The Cause responsible for bringing the universe into existence is not constrained by cosmic time, that Agent demonstrated an existence above, or independent of cosmic time."
[120] Richard Dawkins. The God Delusion. pp. 184-185.
[121] Paul G. Hiebert. Cultural Anthropology. Baker Book House, 2nd ed., 1983. p. 416. Wilhelm P. Schmidt, The Origin and Growth of Religion, 1931. Andrew Lang, Myth, Ritual and Religion. 1887.
[122] International Encyclopedia of the Social Sciences, 1968. Internet accessed under Wilhelm P. Schmidt 04/06/12. Also Wilhelm P. Schmidt. The Origin and Growth of Religion,.Dial Press, 1931. pp. 78, 170-171. Cited in Don Richardson. Eternity In Their Hearts. Regal Books, Revised 1984. pp. 137-140, and Samuel M. Zwemer. The Origin of Religion. Loizeaux Brothers, 3rd ed. 1945. Zwemer cites additional anthropologists who came to the same conclusion as Schmidt and Lang.
[123] Richard Dawkins. The God Delusion. p. 154. See Michael Denton. Evolution: A Theory In Crisis. Adler & Adler, 1986. pp. 345-347.Michael Denton informs us that the fossil records now indicate the gaps between different divisions in nature are as large as ever and frequently larger today than in the time of Darwin. This is the opposite of what evolutionists expect and require.
[124] Richard Dawkins. The God Delusion. p. 155.
[125] Linus Pauling. Quote at <www.azquotes.com/quote872055>.
[126] William Dembski. Intelligent Design. p. 125. Citing Richard Dawkins. The Blind Watchmaker. Norton, 1986. p. 1.
[127] Richard Dawkins. The God Delusion. p. 159.
[128] Ibid.
[129] Frank Sherwin. "Applying Design Analysis to Microbiome Research." Acts and Facts. Institute for Creation Research. February 2016. p. 16.
[130] William A. Dembski. Intelligent Design. p. 260.

[131] Steven Weinberg cited at the "Cosmic Questions Conference" held at the National Museum of Natural History. Reported in USA Today, "Science", April 20, 1999. p. 9D.
[132] Ibid.
[133] Michael Denton. Evolution: A Theory In Crisis. Adler & Adler, 1985. p. 186.
[134] William A. Dembski. Intelligent Design. p. 125. Citing Francis Crick. What Mad Pursuit. Basic Books, 1988. p. 138.
[135] William A. Dembski. Intelligent Design. p. 125.
[136] Carl W. Giberson. "Bottom -Up Apologist." Christianity Today. May 21, 2002. p. 64-65. Polkinghorne finds from his examination of the texts sufficient reason to believe the resurrection accounts are historical and help "make sense of a world many of his colleagues find pointless and absurd."
[137] John Polkinghorne. "Cosmic Questions Conference." USA Today. p. 9D.
[138] Theism is the belief in a personal God who is the Creator of the universe. Christian Theism means that God being personal, seeks to relate to the persons He has created.
[139] "The New Intolerance." Christianity Today, February 2007. p.2 4.
[140] Paul Copan. Is God A Moral Monster? p. 16.
[141] Charles Colson. "Overheated Rhetoric" Christianity Today. June 2007. p. 80.
[142] Charles Colson & Ann Morse. "Verdict That Demands Evidence." Christianity Today, March 28, 2005. <ChristianityToday.com>. Gives examples showing it is evolutionists who prevent academic freedom and stonewall evidence that invalidates their pet theory.
[143] <hotair.com/archives/2006/9/13>. Also see Ted Baehr "The blind leading the blind." Christian Examiner November 2006. p. 5.
[144] Michael Crowley. "Iraq's Eternal War." Time Magazine, June 30, 2014. p. 20. "But how could the secular west hope to understand cultures in which religion is government, scripture is law and the past defines the present?"
[145] Sam Harris. The End of Faith: Religious Terrorism and the Future of Reason. WW Norton, 2004. p. 34.
[146] Anis Shorrish. Islam Revealed. Thomas Nelson, 1988. pp. 58, 59, 66, 67, 69, 145, 146, 149, 150, 181. Robert Morey. The Islamic Invasion. Harvest House, 1992. p. 197. J.N.D. Anderson. The World's Religion's. Eerdman's Publishing, 1968. pp. 56, 57, 85. Bernard Lewis. What Went Wrong? Harper Collins, 2002. p. 6. Richard Dawkins. The God Delusion. Houghton Mifflin, 2006. pp. 46-49. This list could be greatly extended showing Islam was deliberately developed by Muhammad into a violent and coercive religion.
[147] Richard Dawkins. The God Delusion. pp. 45-49. Though he presents the situation as Christians going after homosexuals, the cases are to prevent Christian groups from being forced to allow homosexuals to take leadership positions in their Christian organizations. Whereas the Muslim case was clearly incited irrationally and dishonestly with intended violent consequences against non-Muslims.

[148] It is important to note that English translations of the Qu'ran often vary slightly in the numbering of verses. So check a few verses before and after the designated verse if it is not the intended verse. There are many additional war verses advocating conquest and putting those who will not submit to Islam to death. One Quran I has a list of verses justifying Jihad against non-Muslims.

[149] Matthew 5:5-12, 16, 38-48; 6:14-15, 21-22; 7:12, 24-27. Luke 6:27-46; 10:30-37. A few examples of such violations of the Christian faith though pursued in the name of Christianity were the Crusades, the Inquisition, the religious wars in Europe, persecution of the Jews and the slaughter of the followers of John Huss in Central Europe and of the Huguenots in France.

[150] The LDS Church known as Mormons is a cult that claims to be Christian but mixes some biblical concepts and terminology with pagan and other religious beliefs. This religion does intend to create a Theocracy in which their church rules the U.S. and eventually all governments. This is one of the many ways the LDS religion parallels Islam.

[151] "The New Intolerance." Christianity Today, Feb. 2007. p. 24.

[152] Benjamin Wiker. "How The World's Most Notorious Atheist changed His Mind." Citizen, Focus On the Family.

[153] Ibid.

[154] Robert A. Morey. The New Atheism p. 36. These include housing restrictions in Atlanta forbidding Bible Studies or prayer meeting in homes without permission from the city. In New York it is illegal to preach on any public property or give out religious literature at public beaches or parks. Such restrictions are expanding.

[155] Robert Morey. The Battle of the Gods. Crown Publications, 1989. p. 3. Also the entirety of D. James Kennedy's book What If Jesus Had Never Been Born?, verifies the enormous extent of positive contributions the Christian faith made to society and culture including our unique freedoms, and individual rights. See Jonathan Hill. What Has Christianity Ever Done For Us?

[156] Bertrand Russell. History of Western Philosophy. Allen & Urwin, 1947. p. 556. Referenced by Philip J. Sampson. 6 Modern Myths About Christianity & Western Civilization. Inter-Varsity Press, 2000. p. 39. See other distortions by Russell pp. 92, 99. Russell's Book Ethics and Politics in Human Society has other fabrications by Russell.

[157] Brooke Borel. "Message Control." Scientific American. October 2017. Vol. 37, No. 4. p. 68. Gene drives increase the chances of characteristics being passed on genetically. Manipulating gene drives is said to possibly increase the possibility of determining or eliminating specific traits from 50% to 90%. <www.technologyreview.com/s/601213/theextinctioninvention>.

[158] Felix Lazarev. "The Anthropological Manifestation." Delivered at the symposium on "Man and the Christian Worldview" at Alushta, Ukraine. May, 2010.

[159] Oleg Nikolenko. From an excerpted record of his statement regarding "The Symposiums" recorded by Georges Carellit. in Truth And Consequences. 2015. pp. 147-148.

[160] Movies and TV are purposively being used by some Directors to erode belief in the Christian faith and in biblical morality. Compare a sit-com from the 1950's, and 1960's, with today's and with each other to see the degeneration in language and behavior advocated and acceptable now. These results are due to deliberate intentions to eliminate the moral foundations of our society.

[161] <en.wikepedia.org/wiki/B.F.Skinner>. Also <biography.com/people/bf-skinner>.

[162] Francis A. Schaeffer. Back To Freedom and Dignity. Inter-Varsity Press, 1972.

[163] Georges P. Carillet. "Symposium on 'Christianity, Humanism, Health' an Introduction." in Truth And Consequences. p. 153.

[164] Ibid. Carillet also stated that, "Christianity provides the moral foundation for a healthy social and political order." This is one actual cause for opposition to the Christian Faith. Carillet added, "Christianity will best promote society's health if it is not trivialized, secularized, privatized or made sectarian, and if it is true to itself as revealed in the Bible." p. 157.

[165] Robert A. Morey. The New Atheism And the Erosion of Freedom. p. 36-37.

[166] See the example of Jesus, Matthew 22:23-32 and the apostle's teachings Titus 1:9-11 & 1Peter 3:15-16.

[167] A few of those atheists who have come to faith in Christ in the twentieth century are: G.K. Chesterton, Emile Cailliet, Cyril Joad, C.S. Lewis; Ignace Lepp, Boris Dotsenko, Alister McGrath, Patrick Glynn, Lee Strobel, Sergie Golovin, Vladislov Olkhovsky.

[168] Alister McGrath & Joanna Collicutt McGrath. The Dawkins Delusion? p. 15.

[169] Patrick Glynn. God: The Evidence. Prima Publishing, 1997; Werner Keller. The Bible As History. Morrow & Co., 1957; Lee Strobel. The Case For Christ. Zondervan, 1998. The Case For Faith. Zondervan, 2000. The Case For A Creator. Zondervan, 2004; Lambert Dolphin Jr. Conquest Of Inner Space. Good News Pub., 1969. See also the writings of Alister McGrath, Francis Schaeffer, Josh McDowell & Werner Gitt in the Bibliography.

[170] Andrew Johnson. "Is Christianity Rational." The Humanist. December 2003. p. 39.

[171] Ibid.

[172] The following indicate that Jesus claimed and verified that He was God: Jesus claimed to be the Lord of the Sabbath (Luke 6:5), established by God in Exodus 20; He claimed to forgive sin, the prerogative of God alone (Matt. 9:2-6); He claimed the Hebrew scriptures were about Himself, (Luke 24:27,44); and that Moses wrote about Him (John 5:46); He also claimed to be the I Am (the eternally existent God) of Exodus 3:14-15 (John 8:58). He exercised control over nature (Luke 8:24-25), over disease (Luke 5:12-13), paralysis (Luke 5:24-25) and over death (Luke 7:12-15). Jesus accepted worship (Matt. 8:2; 9:18; 14:33; 15:25; 20:20; 28:9, 17; John 9:38).

[173] Textual Criticism is the process of comparing the ancient manuscripts, quotations of the documents in other writings, and the earliest translations in order to determine the original reading of the documents. The New Testament is certain in more than 98% of the text. No disputed text involve a major teaching.

[174] Andrew Johnson. "Is Christianity Rational?" p. 39.

[175] See F.F. Bruce. The Canon of Scripture. Inter-Varsity Press, 1988; F.F. Bruce. The New Testament Documents: Are They Reliable? IVP, 1960; Craig Blomberg. The Historical Reliability of the Gospels. IVP, 1987; Neil R. Lightfoot. How We Got The Bible. Baker Books, 3rd ed., 2003. Esp. chapters 8-10.

[176] William Ramsey. The Bearing of Recent Discovery On the Trustworthiness of the New Testament. Hodder & Stroughton, 1920. pp. 85, 89. "Further study showed that the book [Acts] could bear the most minute scrutiny as an authority for the facts of the Aegean World, and that it was written with such judgment, skill, art and perception of truth as to be a model of historical statement." A few pages later he added, "You may press the words of Luke in a degree beyond any other historians and they stand the keenest scrutiny and hardest treatment." (p. 89) Ramsey began completely confident that Luke was hopelessly unreliable. See also Ramsey's St. Paul-the Traveler and Roman Citizen; Werner Keller. The Bible As History. William Morrow, 1956 & I. Howard Marshall. Luke: Historian and Theologian. Zondervan, 1970.

[177] Ignace Lepp. Atheism In Our Time. p. 49.

[178] Ibid. p.58.

[179] Alister McGrath. The Twilight of Atheism. p. 26. Also on p. 25 former atheist McGrath mentions that atheists tend to quote one line of Voltaire out of context making it "appear that he was a precursor of Freud's view of God as wish fulfillment."

[180] J. Parton. Life of Voltaire. Vol. 2. Houghton and Mifflin & Co., 1884. p. 554. Cited in Michael Caputo. God Through the Eyes of the Greatest Minds. Howard Publishing, 2000. p. 68.

[181] Ibid. p. 25.

[182] Ibid. p. 27. See also pages 25-26.

[183] Antony Flew. There Is A God. Harper Collins, 2007. pp. 1, 3. Further explained in pages 83-160. Also see the book review by Matt Kaufman. Citizen. Focus On the Family. February 2008. p. 12-13.

[184] Antony Flew. There Is A God. p.88.

[185] Joseph Bayly. "Does Man Exist?" His Magazine. February, 1964. pp. 9-10.

[186] Werner Keller. The Bible As History. William Morrow & Co., 1957. p. xxiii. "In view of the overwhelming mass of authentic and well attested evidence now available, as I thought of the skeptical criticism which from the eighteenth century onward would fain have demolished the Bible altogether, there kept hammering in my brain this one sentence, 'The Bible is right after all.'"

[187] Jack Finegan. Light From The Ancient Past: The Archaeological Background of the Hebrew-Christian Religion. Princeton University Press, 1946. Jack P. Lewis. Archaeological Backgrounds to Bible People. Baker Book House. 1971. Randel Price. The Stones Cry Out. Harvest House, 1997. William M. Ramsay. St. Paul The Traveler and Roman Citizen. Baker Books, reprint 1962. Howard Vos. Genesis and Archaeology. Moody Press, 1963. Clifford Wilson. The Impact of Ebla on Bible Records. Word of Truth Productions, 1977.

[188] Richard Purtill. Thinking About Religion. Prentice Hall, 1978. pp. 84-85.

[189] Robert A. Morey. The New Atheism And the Erosion of Freedom. p. 31.

[190] Ibid. p. 32. See books previously listed in *end notes* for specific examples.

[191] Robert A. Morey. The New Atheism And the Erosion of Freedom. p. 32. Morey further states that at least 90% of attacks on the Bible's credibility and authenticity were based upon arguments from silence rather than evidence or valid argument.

[192] Bill T. Arnold & Bryan E. Beyer. "Exodus: A Miraculous Escape." Encountering The Old Testament. Baker Books, 1999. pp. 103-115. Manfred Bietak. "Exodus Evidence." Biblical Archaeology Review, May/June 2016. Vol. 42, No. 3. pp. 31-37. James K. Hoffmeier. "Out of Egypt: The Archaeological Context of the Exodus." Biblical Archaeological Review. January/February 2007. Vol. 33, No. 1. Kevin D. Miller. "Did the Exodus Never Happen?" Christianity Today. Sept. 7, 1998.

[193] Roy B. Zuck. "Is The Bible True?" American Tract Society, 2002. p. 4. See Josh McDowell. New Evidence That Demands a Verdict. Thos. Nelson, 1999. p. 439.

[194] Roy Abraham Varghese. "Preface" in Antony Flew. There Is A God. p. xxiv.

[195] Joe Aguirre. "Finding Reasons to Believe." The OC Christian Magazine. n.d. (acquired Sept/Oct 2013). p. 10.

[196] Ravi Zacharias. The Real Face of Atheism. pp. 44-45.

[197] Ibid. p. 43.

[198] This should remind you of Darwin's confident but unfulfilled expectation that the fossil record would confirm his theory, and Weinberg's assertion that someday science will explain the universe, order and religious experience better than religion. These beliefs are held by blind faith despite evidence against them.

[199] Kenneth D. Boa & Robert M. Bowman Jr. 20 Compelling Evidences That God Exists. River Oak Publishing, 2003. p. 28.

[200] C.S. Lewis. "De Futilitate" in Christian Reflections. (ed.).Walter Hooper. William B. Eerdmans, 1967. Related to the idea that our perceptions are illusions, Lewis wrote that to assume our minds originated from mindless matter is not an explanation. That," Unless all we take to be knowledge is an illusion, we must hold that in thinking we are not reading rationality into an irrational universe but responding to a rationality with which the universe has always been saturated." pp. 64-65.

[201] Josh McDowell & Don Stewart. Understanding Secular Religions. pp. 30-31.

[202] Ibid, p.31. Referencing Norman Geisler & Paul Feinberg. Introduction To Philosophy. Baker Book House, 1980. p. 296.

[203] C.S. Lewis. "Religion: Reality or Substitute?" in Christian Reflections. p. 41.

[204] C.S. Lewis. "De Futilitate" Christian Reflections. pp. 65-70. "An accusation always implies a standard. And while you are making the accusation you have to accept the standard as a valid one. If you begin to doubt the standard you automatically doubt the cogency of your accusation…If nothing is certainly right, then of course it follows that nothing is certainly wrong."

[205] Kyle Butt & Dave Miller. "The Problem of Evil." Reason & Revelation Vol. 29, No. 6. June 2009. Citing C.S. Lewis. Mere Christianity. Simon & Schuster, 1952. p. 45.

[206] Gen. 3:17-18; 5:29; Romans 8:19-22. These and other Biblical passages indicate that all death, decay and destruction resulted from the fall, human rebellion. This includes genetic problems to weather patterns and entropy in the cosmos.

[207] C.S. Lewis. The Problem of Pain. Fontana Books, 1949. Philip Yancey. Where Is God When It Hurts? Zondervan Corporation, 1977. Paul E. Billheimer. Don't Waste Your Sorrows. Bethany House Pub., 1977. Philip Yancey. Disappointment With God. Zondervan Publishing, 1988. Paul Brand & Philip Yancey. The Gift of Pain. Zondervan Publishing House, 1993. Kyle Butt & Dave Miller. "The Problem of Evil." Reason & Revelation. Vol. 29, No. 6. June 2009. pp. 44-47.

[208] G.K. Chesterton. Orthodoxy. Fontana Books, 1961. p. 15.

[209] Ibid.

[210] Robert A. Morey. The New Atheism. p. 45. A universal negative is a proposition that denies something of all members of a class or category. The statement, 'There is no God' rules out all examples or alleged members of the category 'God' and therefore is a universal negative. Therefore the statement cannot be ruled out by logic.

[211] Deuteronomy 4:29; 2Chronicles 15:2; Isaiah 55:6-7; Jeremiah. 29:13. See also Jesus' words "If any one chooses to do God's will he will find out whether my teaching comes from God or whether I speak on my own." John 7:17 (NIV).

[212] Hugh Ross. Why The Universe Is the Way It Is. Baker Books, 2008. p. 20.

[213] C. Steven Evans. Philosophy Of Religion. Inter-Varsity Press, 1982. p. 124.

[214] Psalm 19:1-6; Isaiah 42:5; 45:12, 18; Romans 1:20.

[215] C.S. Lewis. "Religion and Rocketry." The World's Last Night. Harcourt Brace Jovanovich, Inc.1960. p. 83.

[216] Ibid.

[217] Ecclesiastes 3:11; Job 5:9; Rom. 11:33.

[218] C.S. Lewis. "Dogma and the Universe." Walter Hooper (ed.). God in the Dock: Essays on Theology and Ethics. Eerdmans Publishing, 1970. p. 40.

[219] C.S. Lewis. "Religion and Rocketry." p. 84.

[220] Jake Hebert. "Thick Ice Sheets: How Old Are They Really?" Act and Facts. Institute For Creation Research, June 2015. p. 15.

[221] For example the number of layers deposited in any one year is dependent upon the number of snowstorms for that year. This is impossible to know in regard to past centuries. Glaciologists must guess how many layers have been deposited in any given year in order to come up with an age for the ice sheets. Other methods are also based upon assumptions that cannot be verified.

[222] I. Ebersberger. et. al. "Genomewide Comparison of DNA Sequences Between Humans and Chimpanzees" American Journal of Human Genetics. 2002. 70(6) 1490-1497.

[223] William Dembski. Intelligent Design. Inter-Varsity Press, 1999. p. 261.

[224] John Raymond Hand. Am I Intelligent? Moody Press, n.d. (1938). p. 46.

[225] Jerry Bergman. "Do Any Vestigial Structures Exist in Humans?" CEN Technical Journal .14 (2) 2000. p. 95.

[226] William Dembski. Intelligent Design. p. 150.

[227] Jerry Bergman. "Do any vestigial structures exist in humans? p. 95.

[228] Francisco Ayala. Darwin's Gift to Science and Religion. Joseph Henry Press, 2007. p. 91. Cited by Randy J. Guliuzza. "Our Useful Apppendix-Evidence of Design, Not Evolution." in Acts and Facts. Institute of Creation Research. February, 2016. p. 13.

[229] Duke University Medical Center. "Appendix Isn't Useless At All: It's a Safe House For Bacteria." Science Daily. <sciencedaily.com> October 8, 2007. Cited by Randy J. Guliuzza. "Our Useful Appendix-Evidence of Design, Not Evolution." in Acts and Facts. Institute of Creation Research. February, 2016. p. 13.

[230] Loren G. Martin. "What is the Function of the Appendix? Did It Once Have a Purpose That Has Been Lost?" Scientific American. Oct. 21, 1999. Reprinted <www.scientifamerican.com/article/what is the function of>.

[231] Walter and Eliza Hall Institute. "Immune Cells Make Appendix Silent Hero of Digestive Health." Science Daily. <sciencedaily.com> November 30, 2015. p. 13.

[232] William Parker cited at <rationalthinkerscafe.wordpress.com/2012/07/20/istheappendixuseless/>, stated, "Maybe it's time to correct the textbooks. Many Biology texts today still refer to the appendix as a 'vestigial organ.'" The article adds that recent scientific research indicates the appendix serves important immune functions.

[233] Jerry Coyne. Why Evolution Is True. Viking Press, 2009. pp. 60-61. Cited in Acts and Facts. February 2016. p. 14.

[234] Jerry Bergman. "Do any vestigial structures exist in humans? p. 95.

[235] Ibid.

[236] Ibid. Referencing I. Asimov. Words of Science. Signet Reference Books, 1959. p. 30.

[237] <coccygectomy.org/2010/05/what-is-the-coccyx-and-what-does-it-do/> See also William A. Dembski. Intelligent Design. p. 150.

[238] Jerry Bergman. "Do any vestigial structures exist in humans?" CEN Technical Journal. 14 (2) 2000. p. 96.

[239] Maciej Giertych. "Professor of Genetics Says 'No' to Evolution." Printed from Answers in <Genesis.org> June 1, 1995.

[240] Ibid. When the paired genes for a trait inherited from one parent differs from the one from the other they are called alleles. It is an alternative form of a gene, or result of a mutation.

[241] Discovery Institute staff. <www.discovery.org>. Citing Lee Spetner. Not By Chance. Judiaca Press, 1998.

[242] P.P. Grasse. Evolution of Living Organisms. Academic Press, 1977. p. 217. Translation from the French cited by Alan Hayward. Creation and Evolution. Betany House Publishers, 1985. p. 25.

[243] Ibid.

[244] Maciej Giertych. In the "Forward" of Gerald J. Keane. Creation Rediscovered. Tan Books, 1991. Cited at <creation.com/genetics-has-no-proofs-for-evolution-leading-geneticist>.

[245] Michael Denton. Evolution: A Theory In Crisis. pp. 84-86.

[246] Ibid. pp. 86-87.

[247] Ibid. p. 77.
[248] <Amazon.com/notchance-shattering_modern_evolution>. R.C. Slater. "Evolution: Science or Religion?"
[249] Ibid.
[250] D. M. Mackay. "Is There Still Room For God?" Inter-Varsity Magazine. Intro Issue, 1964. n.p. #. The whole idea of a God of the gaps (thinking that whatever science had not explained still left room for God) was totally erroneous from its inception. Science only explains what occurs not why it does or how it originated. All of the universe, including what science has discovered about its operation, shows the glory and greatness of the God who created and sustains it Psalm 19; Col. 1:16-7; Heb. 1:3.
[251] Jerry Bergman. "Rymond Damadian, Inventor of the MRI." Acts & Facts. Vol. 44, No. 5. May 2015. p. 19.
[252] D.M. Mackay. "Is There Still Room For God?" pp. 1-3.
[253] Interview with Louw Alberts. "Evolution and Creation: A Ranking Scientist Talks About Both." Decision Magazine. March, 1989. p. 23.
[254] Richard L. Purtill. Thinking About Religion. Prentice-Hall, 1978. p. 30.
[255] Geoffrey Berg. The Six Ways of Atheism. pp. 9, 11.
[256] Ibid.
[257] C. Steven Evans. Philosophy Of Religion. p. 128.
[258] See Don Richardson. Lords of the Earth. Regal Books, 1977. For a much broader presentation of the positive impact and influence of Christianity see Jonathan Hill. What Has Christianity Ever Done For Us? Inter-Varsity Press, 2005.
[259] Interview with Louw Alberts. "Evolution and Creation: A Ranking Scientist Talks About Both." Decision Magazine. p. 23.
[260] C. Steven Evans. Philosophy Of Religion. pp. 128-129.
[261] Ignace Lepp. Atheism In Our Time. p. 35.
[262] Martin Buber. Eclipse Of God. Harper & Brothers, 1952. pp. 69-70.
[263] John Blanchard. Is Anybody Out There? p. 9.
[264] Geoffrey Berg. The Six Ways of Atheism. p. 9.
[265] Robert Dick Wilson. A Scientific Investigation of the Old Testament. Moody Press, 1959; F.F. Bruce. The New Testament Documents: Are they Reliable? Inter-Varsity Press. 5th ed., 1960; Warner Keller. The Bible As History. William Morrow, 1966; Norman L. Geisler & William E. Nix. From God To Us. Moody Press, 1974; John W. Haley. Alleged Discrepancies of the Bible. Whitaker House, (Reprint) 1992; Josh McDowell. New Evidence That Demands A Verdict. Thomas Nelson, 1999; Hershal Shanks. The Mystery and Meaning of the Dead Sea Scrolls. Random House. 1999: Eta Linnemann. Historical Criticism of the Bible. Kregal Publications, 2001; Walter C. Kaiser Jr. The Old Testament Documents. Inter-Varsity Press, 2001; Neil R. Lightfoot. How We Got the Bible. Baker Books, 3rd ed. 2003; K.A. Kitchen. On The Reliability of the Old Testament. Eerdman's Publishing Co., 2003.
[266] Dennis Swift. Secrets of the Ica Stones and Nazca Lines. Self-Published, 2006. See also information in the TV special, "Mysterious Origin of Man." Referred to in a following *endnote*.

[267] Guillermo Gonzalez & Jay W. Richards. The Privileged Planet. Regnery Publishing, Inc., 2004

[268] <en.wikipedia.org/wiki/guillermo_Gonzalez_(astronomer)>; and <EvolutionNews.org> July 20, 2007.

[269] Bill Cote. "Mysterious Origin of Man." NBC Documentary. February 25 & June 8, 1996. <http://bcvideo.com/bmom31.html>

[270] Virginia Steen-McIntyre. "Suppressed Evidence For Ancient Man in Mexico." <http://pleistocenecoalition.com/steenmcintyre/Nexus_article.pdf> August-September, 1998.

[271] <en.wikipedia.org/wiki/index.html?curid=7651728>. Biostratigraphic researcher Sam Van Landinham published two peer reviewed articles, 2004 [Micropaleontology Vol. 50, No. 4. pp. 313-342] and further confirmation in 2006 [Journal of Paleolimnology. Vol .36, No. 1. July 2006. Pp. 101-116] justifying Steen-McIntyre's conclusions.

[272] <en.wikipedia.org/wiki/immaneul_velikovsky>

[273] <http://www.knowledge.co.uk/velikovsky/index.htm> The excuse to hinder publication and access to the book is probably best revealed by this excerpt from the book's own preface: "The historical and cosmological story of this book is based in the evidence of historical texts of many peoples round the globe, on classical literature, on epics of the northern races, on sacred books of the people of the Orient and Occident, on traditions and folklore of primitive peoples on old astronomical inscriptions and charts, on archaeological finds and also on geological and paleontological material."

[274] <http://www.amazon.com/Worlds-Collision-Immanuel-Velikovsky/dp/1906833117#reader_1906833117>

[275] <http://www.knowledge.co.uk/velikovsky/index.htm>

[276] Ibid.

[277] Ibid.

[278] Ibid.

[279] Lori Arnold. "'Expelled' documentary explores Darwin, Intelligent Design, religion debate." Christian Examiner. April 2008. p. 6. Information also available at <www.discovery.org/csc/freespeechEvolCampMain.php>

[280] <zoominfo.com/p/Nancy_Bryson/17762029>; <creationwiki.org/Nancy_Bryson>. She feels that none of the origin of life scenarios presented by evolution hold up to scrutiny.

[281] Lori Arnold. "'Expelled' documentary explores Darwin, Intelligent Design, Religion Debate." Christian Examiner. April 2008. p. 6.

[282] David Klinghoffer. "The Branding of a Heretic." Wall Street Journal. January 28, 2005. <wsy.com/articles> & Michael Powell. "Editor Explains Reasons for Intelligent Design Article." Washington Post. August 19, 2005.

[283] <Richardsternberg.org> "Because Dr. Meyer's article presented scientific evidence for intelligent design in biology, I faced retaliation, defamation, harassment, and a hostile work environment at the Smithsonian's National Museum of Natural History that was designed to force me out as a research associate there. These actions were taken by federal government employees acting in concert with an outside advocacy group, the National Center for Science Education. Efforts were

also made to get me fired from my job as a staff scientist at the National Center for Biotechnology Information." This proves that the scientific elite want no alternative to evolution to be published because it reveals their cover-up and censorship of information.

[284] Claudia Wallis. "The Evolution Wars." Time. August 15, 2005. p. 28. (pp. 27-35).
[285] Ibid. p. 32.
[286] Logan Paul Gage. "Deconstructing Dawkins." Christianity Today. Nov. 2007. p. 80.
[287] Richard Dawkins. The God Delusion. p. 34.
[288] Roy Abraham Varghese. "Preface" to Antony Flew. There Is A God. pp. xxii-xxiii. See also the article on Einstein in the Epoch Times. March 23, 2008.
[289] Walter Isaacson. "Einstein & Faith." Time, April 16, 2007. p.46-47.
[290] Ibid. In that interview Einstein also said, *"I believe in Spinoza's God, who reveals himself in the lawful harmony of all that exists, but not in a God who concerns himself with the fate and doings of mankind."* p.47.
[291] Michael Denton. Evolution: A Theory In Crisis. p. 86. Denton continued: "The German zoologist, Bernard Rensch, was able to provide a long list of leading authorities who have been inclined to the view that macroevolution cannot be explained in terms of microevolutionary processes, or any other currently known mechanisms."
[292] Henry Schaaefer. Cited in "A Critique of PBS's Evolution." <reviewevolution.com/press/pressrelease_100scientists.php>
[293] Claudia Wallis. "The Evolution Wars." Time. p. 32.
[294] David Klinghoffer. "The Branding of a Heretic." Wall Street Journal. January 28, 2005. <wsy.com/articles> & Michael Powell. "Editor Explains Reasons for Intelligent Design Article." Washington Post. August 19, 2005.
[295] Michael Denton. Evolution: A Theory In Crisis. p. 75.
[296] Ibid.
[297] Thomas Woodward. Doubts About Darwin: A History of Intelligent Design. Baker Books, 2003. p. 69.
[298] Phillip E. Johnson. Darwin On Trial. Inter-Varsity Press, 2nd Ed., 1993. p. 13.
[299] Thomas Woodward. Doubts About Darwin. p. 72.
[300] Thomas Woodward. Doubts About Darwin. p. 72. This wording was in an early draft of Darwin on Trial Woodward read, but was not included in the published version.
[301] Thomas Kuhn. The Structure of Scientific Revolutions. 2nd ed. University of Chicago Press, 1970. p. 151. Cited by William A. Dembski Intelligent Design, p. 300.
[302] C.S. Lewis. "On Obstinacy In Belief." The World's Last Night and Other Essays. p. 14: "I do not see that the state of 'proportioning belief to evidence' is anything like so common in the scientific life as has been claimed." The Financial Times of London had an article talking about serious cases of academic misconduct including reputable academic journals publishing fake stem cell research and fraudulent data regarding a cancer drug." 5/12-13 2007.
[303] Thomas Paine. The Age of Reason. Thomas Paine Foundation, n.d. p. 33.

[304] Lawrence Krause. A Universe From Nothing. Free Press, 2012. Reference by Jake Hebert. "The Greatest Story Ever Told." Acts and Facts. Institute For Creation Research, July 2017. p. 13.
[305] Werner Gitt. In The Beginning Was Information. New Leaf Publishing, 2006. p. 37-38.
[306] Paul Davies. The Mind of God, 1952. p. 150. Cited by Britton Weimer & Paul Johnson. Searching For Answers. AMG Publishers, 2003. p. 8.
[307] Weimer & Johnson. Searching for Answers. p. 8.
[308] Mark Ridley. Evolution. Blackwells, 2004. p. 225. Cited by Brian Thomas. "Do Darwin's Finches Prove Evolution?" in Acts & Facts Institute For Creation Research. November 2014. p.17. This college textbook states regarding the changes in finch beaks that "beaks evolving up in some years, down in other years, and staying constant in yet other years—probably results in some kind of stabilizing selection over a long period of time." Changes in the size of finch beaks back and forth is not evidence of the evolving of finches into a higher, more complex form of life. The evidence fails to confirm the claim.
[309] <archive.ncsa.illinois.edu/Cyberia/expandUni.html>
[310] Walter Isaacson. "Einstein & Faith" Time Magazine. April 16, 2007. p. 47.
[311] "Cosmic Design: Scientists and Theologians discover a common ground." U.S. News & World Report, July 20, 1998. p.52. Further on this article stated that, "If nothing else, the theological idea of creation ex nihilo-out of nothing—is looking better all the time as inflation theories (main story) increasingly suggest the universe emerged from no tangible source."
[312] Henry F. Schaefer III. Science and Christianity: Conflict or Coherence? p. 49. Citing Arno Penzias. New York Times. March 12, 1978.
[313] Ravi Zacharias. The Real Face of Atheism. p. 124. Citing Robert Jastrow. God and the Astronomers. Warner Books, 1978. p. 105.
[314] There has been extensive criticism of Physicist Robert Gentry's reports and conclusions regarding the halos from evolutionists. They also criticize him for being a creationist. However since evolutionists criticize and reject even the most obvious evidence contradicting their beliefs it seems reasonable to continue to accept this information as valid.
[315] Lambert T. Dolphin, Jr. The Conquest of Inner Space. Good News Pub., 1969. p. 17. Referencing Robert V. Gentry. "Cosmology and Earth's Invisible Realm." Medical Opinion and Review. Oct., 1967. pp. 64-79. See also Gentry. Applied Physics Letters. Vol. 8, 1968. p. 65; Bulletin American Physics Society. Vol. 12. 1967. p. 32.
[316] Ibid. p. 18.
[317] <answers.com/Q/How_long_did_it_take_the_earth_to_cool_after_it_was_created>
[318] Lambert T. Dolphin, Jr. The Conquest of Inner Space. pp. 18-19.
[319] Ibid. pp. 17-19. & Creation Symposium II. Baker Book House. pp. 68 ff.
[320] Donald Chittick. "Dating the Earth and Fossils" A Symposium on Creation II. Baker Book House, 1970. pp. 67-68. Citing Patrick Hurley. How Old Is the Earth? Doubleday & Co., 1959. p. 12. There is no means of determining the age of the earth from radioactive decay because there is no way of knowing how much radioactive material was here at the beginning.

[321] Patrick Glynn. God: The Evidence. pp. 7-8.
[322] Ibid. pp. 22-23.
[323] Hugh Ross. The Fingerprint of God. Promise Publishing, 2nd ed., 1991. pp. 121-131. On pp. 121-122 Ross explains: "The strong nuclear force coupling constant holds together the particles in the nucleus of an atom. If the strong nuclear force were slightly weaker, multi-proton nuclei would not hold together. Hydrogen would be the only element in the universe. If this force were slightly stronger nuclear particles would tend to bond together more frequently and more firmly. Not only would hydrogen (a bachelor nuclear particle) be rare in the universe, but the supply of the various life-essential elements heavier than iron ... would be insufficient. Either way life would be impossible."
[324] Stephen Hawking. A Brief History Of Time. Bantum Books, revised, 1998. p. 129.
[325] Ibid. pp. 129-130.
[326] Ibid. p. 131. From some of Hawking's statements made elsewhere, it does not appear that he recognizes the full implications of his statements made here.
[327] Patrick Glynn. God: The Evidence. p. 8.
[328] Ibid.
[329] Lee Strobel. "The Evidence of God." American Tract Society, 2004.
[330] J.D. Barrow & F.J. Tipler. The Anthropic Cosmological Principle. Clarendon Press, 1986. Referenced by Vladislav Olkhovsky."Seven Serious Problems and Two Riddles of Science as the Nine Wonders of Life and Their Role in Choosing a Worldview." Paper accompanying his lecture. May, 2007. p. 1.
[331] Vladislav Olkhovsky.
[332] Ravi Zacharias. The Real Face of Atheism. p. 47.
[333] Michael Denton. Evolution: A Theory In Crisis. p. 294.
[334] Michael Denton. Evolution: A Theory In Crisis. p. 324. Dawkins is cited falsely claiming that Darwin showed it was possible for blind physical forces to mimic the appearance of design. R. Dawkins "The Necessity of Darwinism." New Scientist, 94, April 15, 1982. pp. 130-132.
[335] William Dembski. Intelligent Design. p. 98.
[336] Hugh Ross. Why the Universe Is the Way It Is. Baker Books, 2008. p. 39.
[337] Ravi Zacharias. The Real Face of Atheism. p. 46.
[338] Eric Barrett & David Fisher. Scientists Who Believe, Moody Press, 1984. p. 3.
[339] Eric Barrett & David Fisher. Scientists Who Believe, p. 6 also <www.iisusbog.com/page37.htm> and <sermoncentral.com>.
[340] David A. Noebel. The Battle for Truth. Harvest House, 2001. p. 127. Citing Karl Marx. Economic and Philosophical Manuscripts. Referenced in Francis N. Lee Communism Versus Creation. Craig Press, p. 8.
[341] <www.biology-online.org/dictionary/Biogenesis>. Biogenesis Definition: 1. The process by which life forms arise from similar life forms. 2. It asserts that living things can only be produced by other living things and not by any non-living thing.
[342] Hans Zinsaer. Rats, Lice and History. Little Brown & Co. 1963 (reprint). p. 51.

[343] Michael Denton. Evolution: A Theory In Crisis. pp. 260-261.
[344] Ibid. p. 261.
[345] Ron Carlson & Ed Decker. Fast Facts on False Teachings. "Evolution." p. 54. Citing Dr. George Wald. Scientific American.
[346] Ibid. Citing Dr. George Wald in Life: Origin and Evolution.
[347] Vladislav Olkhovsky." p. 1.
[348] Ibid. p. 2.
[349] Ibid. p. 3. Referencing A. Einstein. Physics and Reality. 1936; J.W. Oller. Einstein's Gulf: Can Evolution Cross It? Impact #327 of Institute for Creation Research, 2000. p. 19.
[350] Igor Savich. "Appearance of Reality or Nine Theses on the Evolutionary Worldview." Paper read October 2009 at the symposium on "Man and the Christian Worldview" October 15, 2009. Simferopol, Crimea, Ukraine.
[351] Michael J. Behe. Darwin's Black Box: The Biochemical Challenge To Evolution. The Free Press, 1996. p. 26.
[352] Michael J. Behe. Darwin's Black Box. p. 26. Citing C. Mann. "Lynn Margulis: Science's Unruly Earth Mother." Science, 252. pp. 378-381.
[353] Thomas Woodward. Doubts About Darwin. p. 161. Citing Charles Darwin. Origin of the Species. John Murray, 6th Edition 1859. p. 154.
[354] Michael J. Behe. Darwin's Black Box. p. 24.
[355] Ibid.
[356] Ibid. pp. 39-47, 72-73, 87 etc.
[357] Ibid. p. 176.
[358] Werner Gitt. "What Darwin Couldn't Know." De Brude Hand, 2009. p. 4.
[359] Discovery Institute Staff. "The Science of Information" <www.evolutionarynews.org>. August 21, 2005.
[360] Werner Gitt. In The Beginning Was Information. p. 51.
[361] Werner Gitt. "In the Beginning was Information." Lecture Notes given in Simferopol, Crimea, May 2007. p. 1.
[362] Werner Gitt. "In the Beginning was Information." quote given in the lecture.
[363] Ibid.
[364] Ibid. Conclusion to his notes.
[365] Maciej Giertych. "Professor of Genetics Says 'No' to Evolution."
[366] Michael Behe. Darwin's Black Box. See especially chapter 3.
[367] Michael Denton. Evolution: A Theory In Crisis. pp. 274-307.
[368] Ibid. pp. 274-275.

[369] My undergraduate course textbook in the Physical Sciences informed students early in the Geology section that fossils were dated by the rock strata in which the fossils were found. Many pages later the text stated that the rocks were dated by the fossils found therein. Thus the authors were using circular reasoning. They were assuming the theory was true and then interpreting all the data so that it appeared to support the theory. So they were assuming what needed to be proven and then pretending to have proven it! That is not legitimate science. Many others have since pointed out this deception.

[370] R. Monastersky. "Siberian Rocks Clock Biological Big Bang." Science News, Vol. 144. Sept. 4, 1993. p. 149 cf. Science News. Vol. 145. June 11, 1994. p. 145. Also see Amy Barth. "Fossil Prints Rewrite History" Discover. 01.02 2011 p. 67. Referenced in Carl W. Wilson. True Enlightenment: From Natural Chance to Personal Creator. Andragathia Books, 2011. p. 182.

[371] Carl W. Wilson True Enlightenment. p. 182.

[372] Tom Kemp. "A Fresh Look At the Fossil Record." New Scientist. Vol. 108. December 5, 1985. p. 67. Cited by Henry Morris. "The Vanishing Case For Evolution." Institute for Creation Research. <icr.org> Carl C. Branson, W.A. Tarr & W.D. Keller. Introduction to Geology. McGraw Hill, 1941. p. 349. Referenced in Carl W. Wilson True Enlightenment. p. 181.

[373] Carl C. Branson, W.A. Tarr & W.D. Keller. Introduction to Geology. McGraw Hill, 1941. p. 349. Referenced in Carl W. Wilson. True Enlightenment. p. 181.

[374] Kurt P. Wise. (chapter. 6). J.P. Moreland (ed.). The Creation Hypothesis. Inter-Varsity Press, 1994. p. 220. Cited in Carl W. Wilson True Enlightenment. p. 182.

[375] Michael Denton. Evolution: A Theory In Crisis. p. 186.

[376] Ibid.

[377] Ibid. p. 187.

[378] J.E. O'Rourke. "Pragmatism versus Materialism in Stratigraphy." American Journal of Science. 1976. Vol. 276. p. 51.

[379] R.H. Rastall. "Geology." Encyclopedia Britannica. 1949. Vol. 10. p. 168. Rastall taught Geology at the University of London.

[380] Ibid. p. 292-293. Denton also stated that many contemporary animals still possess their supposedly "primitive" characteristics which contradicts the theory.

[381] Hannington Enoch. Where Did Man Come From? Cited at <couragetotremble.wordpress.com>.

[382] Ibid.

[383] Maciej Giertych. "Professor of Genetics Says 'No' to Evolution." Answers in <Genesis.org> June 1, 1995.

[384] Niles Eldridge. Time Frames. Heinemann, 1986. p. 144. Cited by Philip J. Sampson. 6 Modern Myths. Inter-Varsity, 2000. p. 59.

[385] Michael Denton. Evolution: A Theory In Crisis. p. 192.

[386] Steven Jay Gould. Dinosaur In A Haystack: Reflections in Natural History. Harmony Books, 1995. pp. 127-128.
[387] Ibid. p. 141.
[388] Ibid. p. 142.
[389] Michael Denton. Evolution: A Theory In Crisis. p. 193.
[390] Ibid. p. 308.
[391] Maciej Giertych. "Professor of Genetics Says 'No' to Evolution." Answers in <Genesis.org> June 1, 1995.
[392] David Bouujor. "The Early Evolution of Animals." Scientific American. August 2005. pp. 42-47 & Jessica Ruvlinski. "Mammals Stake Their Place in Jurassic Park." Discover. June 6, 2005. p. 17. Cited in Carl W. Wilson True Enlightenment. p. 182.
[393] Nathaniel T. Jeanson. "Purpose, Progress and Promise, part 7." Acts and Facts. June 2015. p. 10. Jeanson obtained his PhD in cell and developmental biology from Harvard. He also wrote that "The majority of fossils are aquatic creatures, yet nearly all fossils are found on land-as if the land were once under water. In addition the geologic layers in which these fossils reside span entire continents, indicating at least a continent-wide catastrophe as the cause."
[394] Harold G. Koenig. The Healing Connection. Word Publishing, 2000. p. 91.
[395] Patrick Glynn. God The Evidence: The Reconciliation of Faith and Reason in a Postsecular World. Prima Publishing, 1997. pp. 57-58.
[396] Wei-Keung. J. Yeung & Yuk-Chung Chan. The positive effects of religiousness on mental health in physically vulnerable populations: A review on recent empirical studies and related theories. International Journal of Psychosocial Rehabilitation. 11 (2), 37-52. 2007. <www.psychosocial.com>.
[397] Christopher Hall."Holy Health." Christianity Today, Nov,23, 1992. pp. 18-22.
[398] Ibid.
[399] Gurney Williams III. "How Prayer Heals." McCall's Magazine, December, 1998. p. 90. Williams quotes medical researchers and their findings.
[400] T.M. Luhrmann. "The Benefits of Church." The New York Times. April 20, 2013. p. SR9. <http://nyti.ms/Z9VXSy>
[401] Ibid. Luhrmann is a Stanford University Anthropologist.
[402] M. Scott Peck. The Road Less Traveled. Simon & Schuster, 1978. See esp. sections titled "The Baby and the Bath Water" and "Scientific Tunnel Vision." pp. 221-232.
[403] Ibid. p. 223.
[404] Harold G. Koenig. The Healing Connection. p. 93. He summarizes the results pages 93-95.
[405] Ibid. pp. 118-119.
[406] Ibid. p. 131.
[407] Ibid, p. 123.
[408] Ibid. p. 126.

[409] T.M. Luhrmann. "The Benefits of Church."
[410] Mark Stibich. "Religion Improves Health." <www.longeivity.about.com>. Dec.4, 2008.
[411] Ibid.
[412] Robert Davis. "Prayer Can Lower Blood Pressure." USA Today. August 11, 1998.
[413] For an interesting article on this issue, see C.S. Lewis "The Efficacy of Prayer." The World's Last Night and Other Essays. pp. 3-11.
[414] Larry Dossey, M.D. Healing Words. The power of Prayer and the Practice of Medicine. HarperCollins, 1993. p. xv. Reports he was surprised to find hundreds of studies reflecting "good science" that reveal healing prayer "as among the best kept secrets in medical science."
[415] Ibid. pp. xvii-xviii.
[416] Ibid. p. xv.
[417] Charles Colson & Ann Morse. "Verdict That Demands Evidence." <ChristianityToday.com>, March 28, 2005. Citations from Rodney Stark. For The Glory of God. Princeton University Press, 2003.
[418] Michael Denton. Evolution: A Theory In Crisis. p. 345.
[419] Ibid. p. 358.
[420] T. Edward Damer. Attacking Faulty Reasoning. p. 7. See the related comments in this regard previously given on page 41.
[421] Robert A. Morey. The New Atheism And the Erosion of Freedom. p. 45-46.
[422] Ibid. Citing Gordon Stein. An Anthology of Atheism and Rationalism. Prometheus Books, 1980. p. 4.
[423] Ibid. p. 46.
[424] Kirby Anderson. "The New Atheists" Probe Ministries. <Probe.org>
[425] Calvin Miller. A Thirst For Meaning. p. 40.
[426] J. Edwin Orr. 100 Questions About God. Regal Books, 1966. My original source not found but partially reconstructed from his reasoning especially in pp. 39-41.
[427] Matt Kaufman. Review of "There Is A God: How the World's Most Notorious Atheist Changed His Mind." Citizen Magazine. Focus On the Family Publications, February, 2008. p. 13.
[428] Ibid.
[429] Albert Einstein. Cited in The Epoch Times. March 23, 2008. <theepochtimes.com/news>
[430] Cyril Joad. Recovery of Belief. Faber and Faber Limited, 1952. p. 28.
[431] Richard M. Weaver. Idea Have Consequences. p. 171.
[432] Ibid. p. 183.
[433] Ibid. This intent to be one's own God is much more evident today than when Weaver originally wrote.

[434] Remember the examples of falsified evidence listed previously; the invalid scientific arguments such as vestigial organs, mutations being examples of an increase of information in the cells rather than the actual loss of information that occurs; assuming the theory to be true and plugging the fossils in where they are needed; and unprovable assumptions such as the prebiotic soup.

[435] Charles E. Hummel. "Does God Exist?" Span Magazine. IFES, Africa, No. 3, 1964. p. 3. "The Word of God came into history and lived among us: the knowledge of God has its locus in time and space. The character of Jesus Christ mirrors the divine nature. The Christian does not believe in the existence of any nebulous God but in the God revealed by Jesus Christ. This God is the living God, a personal spirit, eternal and infinite in power and wisdom."

[436] For examples see: Lee Strobel. The Case For Christ & The Case For Faith & The Case For A Creator; Gerald C. Tilley. The Uniqueness of the Christian Faith; Chris Wright. The Uniqueness of Jesus; N.T. Wright. Who Was Jesus?

[437] In the New Testament Romans chapter 1:18 ff. informs us of the motivation behind the multiplication of human religions. Psalm 19 and Hebrews 1:1:1-3 summarizes God's revelation of Himself to humanity.

[438] Constancio C. Amen. "Proving God's Existence." The Way, IFES, No. 1, 1966. p. 5.

[439] Emile Cailliet. "The Book That Understands Me." His. April, 1964. pp. 31-32.

[440] C.S. Lewis. Surprised by Joy. Collins, Fontana Books, 1955.

[441] Cyril Joad. Recovery of Belief. Faber and Faber Limited, 1952.

[442] Ignace Lepp. Atheism In Our Time. pp. 33-34.

[443] Joe Musser. A Skeptic's Quest. Here's Life Publishers, 1981.

[444] Boris Dotsenko. "Flight to Faith." In Eric C. Barrett & Dave Fisher. Scientists Who Believe. Moody Press, 1984. p. 1.

[445] Ibid. p. 8.

[446] Ken Ham. "After Communism's Collapse: Creation in the Crimea." Interview with former Geophysicist Sergie Golovin who is now a dedicated Christian apologist and creation advocate.

[447] Lee Strobel. "The Evidence of God."

[448] Patrick Glynn. God The Evidence: The Reconciliation of Faith and Reason in a Postsecular World. p. 1.

[449] Carl F.H. Henry. "Science and the Supernatural." ATS, Abridged from Christianity Today. n.d, n.p. *"For me," Dr. Shaw continues, "The answer is a personal relationship with God freely given by him in response to faith in and commitment to the claims of Jesus Christ."*

[450] Jerry Bergman. "Raymond Damadian, Inventor of the MRI." Acts & Facts, Vol. 44, No. 5. May 2015. p. 19.

[451] Carl F.H. Henry. "Science and the Supernatural." ATS.

[452] Ibid.

[453] Ravi Zacharias. Can Man Live Without God? Word Publishing, 1994. p. 165.

Recommended Bibliography: Books

Dembski, William A. Intelligent Design. Inter-Varsity Press, 1999.
Denton, Michael. Evolution: A Theory In Crisis. Adler & Adler, 1986.
Flew, Antony. There Is A God. Harper Collins, 2007.
Geisler, Norman & Frank Turek. I Don't Have Enough Faith To Be An Atheist. Crossway Books, 2004.
Geisler, Norman & Peter Bocchino. Unshakable Foundations. Bethany House, 2001.
Geisler, Norman & Thomas Howe. When Critics Ask. Baker Books, 1992.
Geivett, Douglas R. & Gary R. Habermas (ed). In Defense of Miracles. IVP, 1997.
Glynn, Patrick. God: The Evidence. Prima Publishing, 1997.
Gonzalez, Guillermo & Jay W. Richards. The Privileged Planet. Regnery Pub., 2004.
Habermas, Gary R. & Michael R. Lincona. The Case for the Resurrection of Jesus. Kregal Publications, 2004.
Johnson, Phillip E. Darwin On Trial. Inter-Varsity Press, 2nd Edition, 1993.
Kennedy, D. James. What If Jesus Had Never Been Born? Thomas Nelson, 2001.
Koenig, Harold G. The Healing Connection. Word Publishing, 2000.
Kumar, Steve. Christianity for Skeptics. Hendrickson Publishers, 1987.
Lewis, C.S. Mere Christianity. Macmillan Publishing, 1960.
Lewis, C.S. Christian Reflections. William B. Eerdmans Pub. Co., 1967.
Lightfoot, Neil R. How We Got the Bible. Baker Books, 3rd ed. 2003.
Lutzer, Erwin. The DaVinci Deception. Tyndale House, 2006.
McDowell, Josh & Don Stewart. Understanding Secular Religions. Here's Life Publishers, 1982.
McDowell, Josh. The New Evidence That Demands A Verdict. Thos. Nelson, 1999.
McGrath, Alister & Joanna McGrath. The Dawkins Delusion? IVP, 2007.
McGrath, Alister. The Twilight of Atheism. Doubleday, 2004.
Morey, Robert A. The New Atheism and the Erosion of Freedom. Presbyterian & Reformed Pub., 1986.
Nash, Ronald H. World-Views In Conflict. Zondervan, 1992.
Schaeffer, Francis A. Back To Freedom and Dignity. Inter-Varsity, 1972.
Schaeffer, Francis A. Escape From Reason. Inter-Varsity Press, 1968.
Schaeffer, Francis A. The God Who Is There. Inter-Varsity Press, 1968.
Schmidt, Alvin J. How Christianity Changed the World. Zondervan, 2004.
Stott, John R. W. Basic Christianity. Eerdmans Publishing 1958.
Strobel, Lee. The Case For Christ. Zondervan, 1998.
Strobel, Lee. The Case For Faith. Zondervan, 2000.
Strobel, Lee. The Case For A Creator. Zondervan, 2004.
Tilley, Gerald C. The Uniqueness of the Christians Faith CBUP, 3rd ed., 2018
Tilley, Gerald C. The Bible : An Introduction. CBUP, 2017.
Woodward, Thomas. Doubts About Darwin. Baker Books, 2003.
Zacharias, Ravi. Can Man Live Without God? Word Publishing, 1994.
Zacharias, Ravi. The Real Face of Atheism. Baker Books, 2004.

Articles, Pamphlets, Internet

Anderson, Kerby. "The New Atheists" Probe Ministries. <Probe.org>
Blanchard, John. Is Anybody Out There? Evangelical Press, 2006.
"Evolution News & Views" Discovery Institute. <www.evolutionnews.org>
Pearcey, Nancy. "The Missing Link That Wasn't: National Geographic's 'Bird Dinosaur' Flew Against the Facts." Human Events, March 10, 2000.
Wells, Jonathan. "National Geographic Ignores the Flaws In Darwin's Theory." Discovery Institute, November 8, 2004.
www.RatioChristi.org "What if Christianity Is Actually True?"

Name/Author Index

Abraham (Patriarch) 58
Acton, John (Lord) 31
Agassiz, Louis 112
Aguirre, Joe 59
Alberts, Louw 76
Amen, Constancio 119
Anderson, Kirby 114
Astruc, Jean 57
Augustin, St. 77
Ayala, Francisco 70
Baker, Roger 5
Bayly, Joseph 55-56
Behe, Michael 10,98,99,102,112
Berg, Geoffry 76,79
Bergman, Jerry 71
Blanchard, John 7,36
Boas, Franz 38
Branson, Carl 103
Bronn, Heinrich George 112
Brown, Charlie (cartoon) 115
Bryson, Nancy 82
Cailleit, Emile 120
Carillet, George 5-6,50,51
Carter, Brandon 91
Chesterton, G.K. 64,120
Conquest, Robert 26
Copan, Paul 43
Coyne, Jerry 71
Crick, Francis 41,59
Crocker, Caroline 82
Damadian, Raymond 75,123
Damer, T. Edward 5,112-113
Darrow, Clarence 21
Darwin, Charles 6,10,40,72,82,86,89,98-100,102-103,107,110-112
Davies, Paul 33,88
David (King) 58
Dawkins, Richard 9,11,27,33,35-40,43-44,75,83-85,93,100,122
Demski, William 10,21,40-41,70,94
Dennet, Daniel 43
Denton, Michael 10,74,83-86,93,96,102,104-107,112, 133 (n.123),143 (n291)
de Vries, Hugo 100
Dirks, Gerhard 121
Dixon, Malcolm 123
Dorsey, Larry 111

Dostoevsky 19,27,49
Dotsenko, Boris 95,121
Durant, Will 11
Eagleton, Terry 35
Einstein, Albert 34,54,83,89,90,98,115-116
Eldredge, Niles 106
Engles, Frederick 17
Enoch, Hanington 105
Feuerbach, Ludwig 17-18,76-77
Flew, Antony 32-33,45,55,58,116
Freud, Sigmund 6,17-18,24,54,76-77,107-108
Galileo 47
Gentry, Robert 91,112
Giertych, Maciej 72-73,101,106,112
Gitt, Warner 10,88,100-101
Glynn, Patrick 92,122
Golovin, Sergie 122
Gonzalez, Guillermo 80
Gould, Steven Jay 68,106-107
Grasse, Pierre-Paul 73
Haeckel, Ernst 20,127 (n.53).
Ham, Ken 22
Harris, Sam 9,25,27,43
Hawking, Stephen 87,92
Hayhoe, Katherine 8
Hazen, Craig 45
Hebert, Jake 68
Hedges, Chris 43
Hitler, Adolph 24,121
Holt, Jim 35
Hubble, Edwin 89-90
Huxley, Aldus 23
Huxley, Julian 74
Isimov, Isaac 71
Jastrow, Robert 90
Joad, Cyril 9,117,120
Johnson, Andrew 52-53
Johnson, Paul 24,25,34
Johnson, Philip 85-86,112
Jung, Carl 24
Keller, W.D. 103
Keller, Werner 57
Kemp, Tom 103
Khrushchev, Nikita 26
Koenig, Harold G. 109-110
Krause, Lawrence 87
Kuhn, Thomas 86

151

Lang, Andrew 38
Larson, David 108
Lawrence, D.H. 24
Lazarev, Felix 48
Lepp, Ignace 15,17,19,54,77,121
Lewis, C.S. 12,35,62,67,120
Luke, St. 53,56
McDowell, Josh 12,121
McGrath, Alister 9,12,14,25,28,51-52, 54-55,122
McIntyre, John A. 124
McIntyre, Virginia Steen 80-81
Mackay, D.W. 74
Margulis, Lynn 98
Martin, Loren 70
Marx, Karl/marxist 6,12,15,17-18,20,27 54,76,77,95,96,121
Meyer, Stephen 10,82,84,131(n100)
Miller, Calvin 6,32
Morey, Robert A. 20,22,34,47,51,57,113
Moses 58-59
Muhammad 44
Mulinhill, Paudge 7
Mussolini, Benito 24
Newall, Norman 103
Nietzsche, Frederick 17-18,24-26, 28-29,53,78
Nikolenko, Oleg 48
Novak, Michael 35
Nye, William 22
O'Donnel, Rosie 43
O'Keefe, John A. 92
O'Rourke, J.E. 104
Olkhovsky, Vladislav 92,96-97
Orr, J. Edwin 114-115
Owen, Richard 111
Packer, James I. 14-16,24
Paine, Thomas 87
Parker, William 71
Pasteur, Louis 95
Paul, St. 56
Pauling, Linus 39
Peck, M. Scott 109
Penzias, Arno 90
Pictet, Francois Jules 111
Plank, Max 87
Polkinghorne, John 41,92-93
Ross, Hugh 10,37,66,91,94
Russell, Bertrand 39,47

Sandage, Alan 90
Sartre, John-Paul 17,53,78
Savich, Igor 97
Schaeffer, Francis 32,50
Schaeffer III, Henry F. 10,84
Schmidt, Wilhelm P. 38,126(n31)
Scopes, John (trial) 21,127(n56)
Shatunovskaya, Olga 26
Shaw, George Bernard 24
Shaw, James H. 123
Skinner, B.F. 49-50
Slipher, Vesto 89
Socrates 13
Spetner, Lee 73-74
Stalin, Joseph 24
Stark, Rodney 111
Stein, Gordon 113
Steinberg, Milton 23
Sternberg, Richard 82-83,142(n283)
Stibich, Mark 110
Strobel, Lee 121
Strunk, Orlo 30
Swift, Dennis 79
Tarr, W.A. 103
Varghese, Roy Abraham 32-33,58-59
Velikovsky, Immanuel 81-82,112, 142(n273)
Voltaire 12,19,54-55
Wald, George 97
Wallace, Claudia 83
Wallace, Lew 120
Weaver, Richard 28-29,117
Weiner, Norbert 101
Weinberg, Steven 40-43
Wells, Jonathan 10, 127(n54,55)
Wills, Garry 43-44
Wilson, Carl 103
Wise, Kurt 103
Woodward, Thomas 85
Zacharias, Ravi 24,60-61,124
Zinsaer, Hans 96

Printed in Great Britain
by Amazon